COUNSELING
FOR THE
LIBERAL ARTS
CAMPUS

[handwritten: Symposium on]

Counseling for the Liberal Arts Campus

THE ALBION SYMPOSIUM

Held on the campus of Albion College, Albion, Michigan, October 31 to November 2, 1967. Supported by the Danforth Foundation.

edited by JOSEPH C. HESTON
and WILLARD B. FRICK

THE ANTIOCH PRESS • 1968

Copyright © *1968*
by *The Antioch Press*
Yellow Springs, Ohio 45387
Library of Congress Catalog Card Number 68-19531
Manufactured in the United States of America

Preface

We are happy to serve as editors of the proceedings herein reported. They represent the fruition of many plans and much effort on the part of numerous people. We have been pleasantly reassured by the Symposium participants that these plans and efforts were eminently worthwhile. Perhaps the vitality and significance of those three days at Bellemont Manor will in some way permeate the pages of this report. We hope that these materials will serve as an inspiration and guide to those responsible for developing or improving student counseling facilities on the small college campus.

Before we became editors, we were first dreamers and then planners. The idea of the Symposium "just growed" like Topsy in *Uncle Tom's Cabin* out of our feelings of counseling needs for the private liberal arts campus. When our own campus endorsed the plan, we took it to the Danforth Foundation. They not only generously agreed to underwrite our proposal, but encouraged expansion of its scope. Their support was financially essential and sound encouragement for the basic idea of the Symposium.

Our personal thanks for the success of the endeavor go to many people. First, President Louis W. Norris of Albion College not only put the resources of the school behind the project, but also gave the symposium his personal support by full attendance at all its sessions. Dr. Laura Bornholdt, of the Danforth Foundation, helped in securing their favorable approval. Mr. Darrell Beane, now of Earlham College, was then at Albion and extremely helpful in formulating the proposal for submission to the Danforth Foundation. Mr. Harry Berg and Mr. Tom O'Meara, of Albion College's Bellemont Manor, were much appreciated hosts in their handling of housing, meals, and physical facilities. Mr. George Race, our electrical technician, did the video-tapes and sound recordings for every Symposium session—fifteen hours of excellent tapes. Mrs. Dean Dooley, research assistant in our BIRC office, has had the demanding and, at times, difficult task of transferring taped sound to typed copy. Mr. Paul Rohmann of The Antioch Press very helpfully supervised the final emergence of the printed volume. To all these fine people our sincere thanks and heartfelt appreciation.

December 1967　　　　　　　　　　　　　　　　　　JOSEPH C. HESTON
　　　　　　　　　　　　　　　　　　　　　　　　　　WILLARD B. FRICK

Bureau of Institutional Research and Counseling
Albion College

Contents

Preface   v

INTRODUCTION

Background, Purpose, and Program of the Symposium—
Joseph C. Heston, Willard B. Frick   3

ADDRESSES

The Role of Alienation in Identity Formation of College
Students—*Edward S. Bordin*   8

Some Problems and Proposals in College Counseling—
C. H. Patterson   24

An Emerging Morality and the College Counselor—
Lester A. Kirkendall   45

Counseling for Healthy Personality—*Sidney M. Jourard*   72

PANEL PRESENTATION
EDUCATIONAL-VOCATIONAL GUIDANCE

Extent of the Problem—*Lawrence Riggs*   90

How to Provide Occupational Information and Still Be a
Counselor—*Albert W. Davison, Jr.*   98

Personality Correlates in Educational-Vocational Guidance—
John R. Thompson   104

Using Tests—*Frank B. Womer*   112

Mental Health Issues in Liberal Arts Colleges and Their
Implications for Curricular Development—
William R. Rogers   117

PANEL PRESENTATION
INNOVATIONS AND NEW DIRECTIONS IN COUNSELING

Philosophy and Trends—*Herbert I. Posin, M.D.*   127

The Use of Immediacy in Counseling—*Milton R. Cudney*   132

The College Counseling Center: A Center for Student Development—*Weston H. Morrill, Allen E. Ivey, Eugene R. Oetting*   141

A Systematic Approach to Pre-Marital Counseling—*Aaron L. Rutledge*   158

TOPIC GROUP REPORTS

A. Development and Operation of a Counseling Service   171

B. Psychotherapy with Students   177

C. Mental Health Issues on the College Campus   180

D. Prevention: Techniques and Programs   184

E. "New Morality" on the Campus   188

APPENDIX

Participants in the Symposium   192

COUNSELING
FOR THE
LIBERAL ARTS
CAMPUS

INTRODUCTION

JOSEPH C. HESTON
WILLARD B. FRICK
Albion College

Background, Purpose, and Program of the Symposium

BACKGROUND AND ORGANIZATION

● To learn more about and, hopefully, to help solve a real and increasingly significant problem common to liberal arts colleges—a problem which often seems to be most acute in the academically strongest institutions—the Bureau of Institutional Research and Counseling of Albion College developed a proposal for a three day *Symposium on Counseling for the Liberal Arts Campus*. In December 1966 this proposal was submitted to the Danforth Foundation of St. Louis, Missouri. The Danforth people approved the idea and not only offered to financially support the symposium but proposed to support even more participants than originally requested.

The Symposium was planned for October 31–November 2, 1967. It was held at Bellemont Manor, the Center for Continuing Education at Albion College, Albion, Michigan. Invitations were sent to the thirty-four member colleges of these three regional associations:

GREAT LAKES COLLEGES ASSOCIATION:

Albion College
Hope College
Kalamazoo College
DePauw University
Earlham College
Wabash College

Antioch College
Denison University
Kenyon College
Oberlin College
Ohio Wesleyan University
The College of Wooster

ASSOCIATED COLLEGES OF THE MIDWEST:

Beloit College
Carleton College

Knox College
Lawrence University

Coe College
Cornell College
Grinnell College

Monmouth College
Ripon College
St. Olaf College

CENTRAL STATES COLLEGE ASSOCIATION:

Alma College
Augustana College
Carroll College
Gustavus Adolphus College
Illinois Wesleyan Univ.
Luther College

MacMurray College
Manchester College
Millikin University
Mundelein College
St. John's University
Simpson College

Each member was invited to send its director of counseling (if it had one, or an equivalent person), the dean most closely related to counseling, and the college president. All expenses, except travel costs, were covered by the grant from the Danforth Foundation. All but one of the colleges sent representation, though the the pattern varied considerably. In actual attendance there were 74 delegates from member colleges plus 10 invited speakers. They came from these states: Michigan (14), Indiana (9), Ohio (14), Wisconsin (9), Minnesota (8), Iowa (7), and Illinois (19). The categories of positions represented were: Directors of Counseling or Counselors (20), Deans of Students (20), Deans of Men (8), Deans of Women (9), Academic Deans (5), Chaplains (3), Psychiatrists (3), Psychologists (7), Presidents or Vice-Presidents (6), and Others (3). In addition, four press writers and several photographers attended most of the sessions.

Purpose

The Albion Symposium was noteworthy as a pioneer venture in which these representatives of private colleges of the liberal arts tradition lived closely together for three days to talk about counseling problems, procedures, and objectives. It was indeed a significant learning and sharing experience. On a follow-up evaluation form the great majority of the participants rated it well above their expectation level. These printed pages can provide the factual talks presented and summarize the group discussions. However, they cannot convey the personal interchanges, incidental learnings, and new friendships which were a paramount feature of the whole Symposium experience.

Our plans for the Symposium grew from the awareness that stress factors for college students are multiplying, and that many an institution whose ethos is most productive of the pressures and tensions which contribute to student stress is not presently well equipped to cope with the manifestations and consequences of such stress. Many smaller colleges, in particular, while making major strides in the development of their academic programs and enrolling unusually able student bodies, have not kept pace with larger or more affluent institutions in the development of adequate and appropriate counseling facilities for their students. In the small liberal arts college, especially the institution with a high level of expectancy and academic competition, the need for upgrading counseling services, and for providing opportunities for professional counselors to communicate with each other and with the eminent authorities in the field, has never been greater.

Dr. Dana L. Farnsworth, Professor of Hygiene and Director of University Health Services at Harvard University, underscores the scope of the problem with some alarming forecasts. In his recent book, *Psychiatry, Education, and the Young Adult*, (Charles C. Thomas, 1966), this authority on student mental health problems estimates that for every 10,000 students:

> 1000 will have emotional conflicts severe enough to warrant professional help.
>
> 300 to 400 will have feelings of depression deep enough to impair their efficiency.
>
> 100 to 200 will be completely apathetic, and unable to organize their efforts.
>
> 20 to 50 will be so adversely affected by past family experiences that they will be unable to control their impulses.
>
> 15 to 25 will become ill enough to require hospital treatment.
>
> 5 to 20 will attempt suicide, and 1 to 3 will succeed.

Significant research in this field tends to be concentrated in the larger, generally state-supported universities, which tend, in turn, to dominate the meetings of national associations in which counseling personnel hold membership. A distinct need, often not met in such meetings, is the opportunity for counselors from relatively small liberal arts colleges—colleges often lacking easy access to specialists in the field and in opportunities for their own counseling personnel—to consult with their counterparts from comparable institutions.

It is with these circumstances in mind that the Symposium was arranged. Thus, persons with counseling responsibility at liberal arts institutions in the Midwest met together to listen to and share in discussions of their responsibilities, formally and informally, with each other and with acknowledged authorities in the field. From such sharing of common concerns, new ideas, and resources there should emerge some counseling innovations, procedural improvements, and a clearer understanding of the values and limitations of various types of psychological services on the liberal arts college campus. These pages contain some of our answers. We hope they are only a beginning along these lines.

Program

The specific content of the program is found in the following proceedings. The various speakers were, of course, responsible for the particular ideas in the papers they presented. The editors are responsible for the general nature of the program. This is true because they both arranged the topical format and selected the speakers and panelists to handle each of the segments. The topics, as finally chosen, were the outgrowth of an opinion poll in which a sample of anticipated participants indicated their degree of interest in a variety of suggested topics. Thus, in the last analysis, these are the topics our participants asked us to include.

Four main speakers, all from outside the three regional groups, were invited. Each was chosen on the basis of his familiarity with and stature in the designated topical field. Reaction panels and/or discussion leaders were designated to lead reaction to each of the four main speakers. Advance copies of the talks were given the reactors for their preparatory study.

To encourage further delegate participation, two broad panel topics were arranged. Panelists both from within and without the three associations were chosen and given tentative topics to develop as they wished.

Finally, all participants, member delegates and invited speakers, were assigned to one of five topic discussion groups. Advance topic descriptions and ballots permitted each member to designate his topic group preference. The groups were given broad general areas or topics to explore as they saw fit. They met for three separate hour sessions and were asked to draw up a set of observations and recommendations. These five group reports were then presented to the whole Symposium for discussion in the final morning's sessions.

ADDRESSES

EDWARD S. BORDIN
University of Michigan

The Role of Alienation in Identity Formation in College Students

● Conferences such as this ought to provide opportunities for renewal, occasions for re-examining our assumptions and for broadening our views of colleges and the students who inhabit them. Institutions and students alike are subject to change over time, and college staffs must be alerted to these changes so that they can respond accordingly. In discussing identity formation and alienation in college students, I intend to call to your attention how awareness of changes in the nature of the college student, reflecting his times, must be combined with increased understanding of personality development during the college years to facilitate his learning and growth.

One thing has not changed the significance of college for the entering student. College is simultaneously an extended entry chamber into the adult world and a chance at a last fling, a childlike freedom from responsibility, a moratorium, to use the Eriksonian term. When he enters a college or university, the student is taking important steps toward forging a pattern of living which expresses his values, his integration of his impulses with his resources, his conception of himself, and his community's conception of him. Curricular requirements force him sooner or later to commit himself to a specialization in his studies which implicitly or explicitly defines an occupation. The formal and informal social organization of the college community offers him an opportunity to reopen the question of which subcultural version of the American culture he will make his own. Because affluence brings marriage closer to the college years, relationships between the sexes become a more realistic assessing of partners for the formation of family units. They offer him further opportunities to explore his capacities for forming and enjoying intimate relationships.

In one way or another, more or less successfully, colleges have geared themselves toward these developmental tasks for their students. We have heard much of the conflict between vocationalism and general education, but the realities require that institutions of higher education be concerned with both of these aims. The student's inner nature as well as the persons who surround him exert insistent pressures to settle on a vocation. Yet the student must prepare himself for a life in which the shrinking time needed for productive activities allows him much greater opportunity for relationships with family and friends and ample elbowroom for other uses of his resources. He has to acquire the means to enjoy as rich, as intimate, and as varied a life as our society affords. And with all this, he must clarify and strengthen a philosophy of life, an attitude toward past, present, and future which gives life meaning and provides a base for assuming responsibilities for himself and others. The liberal arts, especially the humanities, are particularly concerned with such aims.

Within this framework, identity formation and alienation would appear to equal good and evil: identity is to be sought and alienation to be avoided. Identity formation seems to mean fitting into our social system, finding one's niche; alienation means dropping out, becoming disaffected, even attacking and destroying. A perusal of headlines supports this view. There are the "good guys," who are dutifully preparing for an occupation and practicing to become upright and conscientious parents and citizens. The "bad guys" challenge the very bases on which we proceed. They ask to lead in decisions we have considered too important to allow them to make—curriculum, grading, and the like. They are the ones who embrace all that we consider harmful or destructive—marijuana, LSD, homosexuality, Maoism. This black and white approach oversimplifies the developmental issues, but first we must take a closer look at what we mean by alienation and whence it comes.

Referents and Sources of Alienation

The word, of course, refers to estrangement, the withdrawing of affection and attachment. Yet some examples of such action are taken for granted and others are damned by applying the term to them.

The fact that a young man is unwilling to pursue his father's occupation or espouse his political or religious views may cause this parent to feel that his son has become alienated from him, but neither he nor the rest of us are likely to equate this with today's *alienated youth*. These are normal breaks from family tradition, within the larger American tradition of class mobility and personal independence. It is when mores and other widely shared social commitments are challenged and rejected that we begin to use the term "alienation." The student who drops out of college, not because he does poorly, but because he is uninterested and questions the point of his studies, is called alienated. Certain violations of social standards fall into the accepted category of "college pranks," but others, which deny the very validity of social controls, earn the pejorative designation.

First, we must ask whether "alienation" is more prevalent today than ever before. A definitive answer must be left to the historians. Certainly, every age has heard challenges to the larger community as well as to the college from its students. During the thirties, large numbers of college students, appalled by the suffering and the human and material waste of the depression, and repelled by the looming clouds of war, espoused radical political movements. Students then challenged current versions of capitalism, political democracy, and foreign policy. In the last half of the nineteenth century students took active roles in wresting control of colleges from the hands of the clergy, in stimulating the substitution of lectures and research activity for the stultifying question and recitation system, and in liberalizing the curriculum. The nineteenth century had its equivalents of social rebellion—it too indulged in mind-expanding experiences, smoking opium with the same religious fervor fanned by Thomas DeQuincy as Timothy Leary has given to indulgence in LSD and, more frivolously, inhaling laughing gas or sniffing ether as a convivial activity.

How is this to be understood? Does it represent universally present archaic destructive forces which can only be ruthlessly stamped out in each generation? I shall argue that alienation is an ingredient of effective identity formation, which contributes to the plasticity of social organization, facilitating adaptation of social structures and procedures to change. "In the process of finding a niche in some section of his society," to use Erikson's words, "the young adult gains an assured sense of inner continuity and social sameness which will bridge what he *was* as a child and what he is *about to become*, and will reconcile his *conception of himself* and his *community's recognition* of him" (3). In doing so he partially repudiates and shapes his childhood identifications that become absorbed into the realities of his person and time. The individual shapes his identity to tune it to his time, but his time is to some degree shaped by him. This intimate relationship between the crystallization of self and social context is reflected in the prominent role that young men and women have played in social change.

Some repudiation of the past, both individual and social, is part of the process of becoming a distinct person. But this individualizing process does not begin during the college period, it only becomes accelerated and crystallized. And it reflects the individual's strengths and weakness. In some patterns of alienation we find evidence of severe mistrust of self and others, of a fearful and wounded withdrawal, and of intense unrealistic anger manifestly directed toward others, often with subtle elements of self-destruction. These are instances in which the phenomena of alienation exceed the requirements of constructive self-affirmation and reflect serious states of maldevelopment. It is a paradox that though we set great store by individual freedom and independence, we are more troubled by those who embrace this ideal too enthusiastically than by those who respond too timidly. To be sure, it was not so long ago that one heard moaning and sighing about the conformist generation of college students. The young person who clings desperately to his models beyond the point of their serving a useful purpose is often presenting difficulties of development of a more insidious nature than his flamboyantly rebellious neighbor.

Finally, we must turn our attention to the influence of the social milieu. I have already intimated that today's college student heard his elder brother criticized for being a conformist without social concern or ideals and only involved with securing a materialistically satisfying future. Today's student is relatively untouched by memories of the widespread economic insecurity of the thirties or the terrifying growth of fascism culminating in world-wide holocaust. But he grew up in the shadow of nuclear threat and brinksmanship. The battle over civil rights gave him an opportunity to have a hand in shaping his world, which may have overcome the feelings of helplessness, of being in the middle while statesmen brandished nuclear thunderbolts of incalculable destructiveness. And now he faces service in a war over which there is deep division of opinion about its methods and goals. It is certainly a period which promotes re-examination of accepted values. Whatever educational excesses may have been perpetrated in the wake of our national response to Sputnik, there has been an acceleration in the intellectual development of our youth. Students are coming to college more widely read than ever before and readier to function with greater intellectual maturity. Just as he seeks a more active role in shaping his larger world, the college student wishes and is ready for a more active part in shaping the college community. He takes our social ideals seriously and is impatient with contradictions and compromises. With minor exceptions he has lived a life in which material wants could be satisfied more readily than ever before, and his parents were made fearful of asserting themselves by experts in child rearing who told them they must be permissive or harm their children. One wonders how much the current generation's mistrust of its elders stems from encounters with parents who had to present their desires and aspirations, and their prohibitions, for their children under the mask of permissiveness.

Facilitating Identity Formation

With this view of the college student and his times, let us turn our attention to how we should structure his environment and what we can do to facilitate his development. First, I will speak of three general stances that I advocate and then will take up more specialized counseling problems.

General Maxims:

At this point I am speaking to teachers, general student personnel workers, and specialized counselors—in short, all those members of the college staff directly concerned with the education of students.

Respect his maturity, but accept his immaturity. For most students the act of entering college creates a new relationship to their parents. Usually the young person no longer lives at home, and often the school is located in a different city. He expects and is expected to assume new responsibilities for himself. The college must be arranged to permit this movement toward adulthood. Yet it is a grave error to assume that he is fully mature and in fact expects to be treated as such. He will seek and even demand greater control over his use of time, decisions about the friends he selects and the studies he pursues. But there will be times when he wants and needs to return momentarily to a more dependent and more nurtured state. Examples are easy to find. Students at the University of Michigan, as in so many other schools, objected to regulations requiring all women students and male freshmen to live in dormitories or other supervised University housing. They claimed the right to go out into a free community market to make their own housing arrangements. But when they achieved a liberalizing of these regulations and moved into the community, the increased competition for this kind of housing brought about rising rents. Now there was a cry for the University to step in to protect them against these rising costs. As another instance, students claim the citizen's right to choose their own forms of protest on the issues of the day, but turn to the University to protect them with legal aid, bail, and the like when their activities run afoul of the law.

The adult's response to such regressions ought not be tinged with the vindictive attitude: "See, you are not as grown up as you think you are"; "You have made your bed, now you must lie in it." I fear that too frequently we neither respect the student's maturity nor accept his immaturity. The college community should be a half-way house for young adults. It should provide them with a base for entering adult responsibility and, where necessary, for protection from their immaturity. I think we sometimes forget that adulthood itself is not without opportunities to rely on others at times when conditions impair the function of our resources or exceed our capacity to cope with them. Learning to accept one's own limitations is facilitated by experiencing acceptance from others.

The challenge for the college is to organize its regulatory processes so that the student takes an important hand in establishing them and at the same time moves toward fuller self-regulation. It means that alongside the social system there has to be a process of individualizing it so that the student who has had to rely a great deal on external pressures will not be abruptly plunged into a situation where he must take full charge of himself. His self-respect requires that the situation be overtly different; he is no longer to be treated as a child. But he must be able to sense an unobtrusive caring about him and a willingness to give aid without derogation, to have the security to test and develop his capacity for using this new freedom.

What holds for the student's social life applies even more for his intellectual life. I have already suggested that college students are more mature intellectually than ever before. Many of them are ready to soar, interacting with their teachers in an active collaboration of equal partners. Yet even these unusual students at some points, and a large number of students at many points, need a more active and supporting teacher who can be encouraging and helpful when the problems of mastery seem especially difficult.

Above all, the student must be given opportunities for honest participation. When he is given responsibilities they ought to be ones that we can allow him to assume. His mistrust of himself and others must not be fed by such devices as self-governing structures in which he is given the appearance of controlling his fate in areas where college administrators feel they must retain the ultimate power. It is better to have an honest confrontation than behind-the-scenes manipulation. But be certain that you have thought through realistically and thoroughly why you must retain this power. Tradition, convenience, and the desire to avoid conflicts with conservative elements of the larger community are too often the factors disclosed by such an examination. Once more the search for identity discloses the need for social change.

Do not take sides with parts of himself. The period of actively crystallizing one's identity is likely to be a period when one is at war with oneself. Infantile attachments exert strong attractions, creating the illusion that going our own way requires giving up all love and affection for those who nurtured us and toward whom we felt so much. It is a time of ambivalence. At one and the same time, the person wishes to stand on his own and looks for and even demands the support of others. He wishes to become a distinct person, yet clings to his earlier, more slavishly followed models. One of the commonest ways of reducing the discomforts engendered by these conflicting feelings is to externalize one side of the conflict. It is father who wishes him to go into accounting, it is a teacher who thinks he is overdoing his social life. The achievement of a stable and mature identity requires that the person come to terms with the impact of his past experiences on him while discarding the infantile husks in which they are embedded. If his life with his parents and their community has embedded certain values, certain methods of delaying and directing his impulses, and these are part of the individual's character, this is a reality of self that must be confronted and modified for present usefulness; and this is best done by divesting these attitudes of their infantile rigidity rather than leaving them untouched by treating them as though they were present external influences. Those who surround him must not be trapped into lending themselves to the student's self-deception. They must be alert to the times when, instead of being external restraints and supports that the students need, they can, by intervening, only serve a regressive purpose of perpetuating the inner conflict.

Help him keep himself open. The difference between being a passive product of the influence of others and an active emerging person lies in the degree to which one's personal stamp is placed on the residue of these influences. Where before, for example, his values were acquired as emotional necessities of his childish dependence on and love for his parents, they must now be reacquired, no doubt in somewhat modified form, based on his growing knowledge and experience and adapted to his motives. His values and moral standards are no longer someone else's precepts; they are truly his own. All varieties of college experience are capable of contributing to this process. Literature, philosophy, history, the physical and biological sciences stimulate his imagination, increase his awareness of inner and outer realities, give him the tools for thinking and acting. He encounters norms of behavior different from his own, and a wide range of individual patterns exhibited by his fellows and by college staff provide him with contemporary models.

The student comes to college expecting to be changed by his experience, yet with reservations about change. He is no different from the rest of us who seek change yet fear the unknown. He avoids change in many ways. In some instances, he simply adopts a new pattern in toto, but only temporarily. In other instances, he learns new ideas by rote instead of coming to grips with their general and personal meanings. It is in this sphere that teachers usually face their greatest challenge. Their task is to bring about a full involvement with the subject.

The Responsibilities of the Psychological Counselor:

The preceding remarks were directed toward teachers and general student personnel workers. We now turn our attention to the contributions of the psychological counselor.

Psychological tests can play an important part in identity formation. They provide a medium through which the individual may confront his growing capacities, his changing values, his modes of coping with anxiety and environmental challenges, and his images of self. Since most colleges have programs of testing all students either at entrance or shortly thereafter, and these responsibilities are often incorporated into the psychological counselor's functions, we should examine them in the light of our preceding discussion. While I am not unaware of the arguments for such group testing programs for admissions and orientation purposes, I am skeptical that all of them are tenable, especially those supporting the latter purpose. One difficulty is that group testing programs make it easy for the student to externalize and compartmentalize the results. It is not a case of his deciding to submit himself to a particular test because he is puzzled about that aspect of himself and so desired a check on his perception of himself. Too often such testing programs are the basis for others doing something to him—admitting him, placing him, deciding whether he ought to be placed on probation, and so on. When interest and personality inventories are included in the test batteries, the current outcry against invasion of privacy can become a source of difficulty. When testing is done as part of the individual's grappling with personal problems or decisions or as a prophylactic self-examination, the issues of invasion of privacy do not occur. Finally, the presence of such group test material provides opportunities for inaccurate conclusions drawn by teachers and others insufficiently acquainted with test technology and may become an inappropriate influence on the teacher's treatment of the student. We will have to re-examine earlier ideas that teachers ought to know their students' levels of ability, aptitudes, and interests in light of recent research on the influence of expectations on outcomes. Many recent studies indicate that expectations of counselors, therapists, and experimenters can influence results. I have seen reports of a newly issued book by Rosenthal (4) which demonstrates that teachers who were led to believe they were teaching exceptional students graded them higher than those who were led to believe that their students were average, and, more importantly, graded students lower when they were led to expect inferior performance. Rather than a means for understanding the students, tests may become agents for fulfilling the prophecies they contain.

Instead of functioning as a dispenser of test information, the psychological counselor will best help the teacher individualize his teaching by acting as a consultant to him. Not only will this enable the teacher to see how his teaching goals and methods interact with the student's search for himself, but it can provide a means for early identification of those students whose maldevelopments are severe enough to require special clinical intervention. The consultative function is one that I fear has been greatly neglected by psychological counselors. Too often we have been bogged down in our offices, because of personal comfort derived from working in this secluded state, a too precious conception of our roles, or because our awkwardness has made unsuccessful our efforts to establish working relationships with others concerned with students. Everyone knows the telling arguments for increasing the effects of the small supply of mental health professionals. We must insure that our presence enhances rather than undermines the teacher's willingness to be concerned with the individual student and to seek to understand the special character of his development so that he can adapt his teaching to it.

The process of establishing and carrying out a consultative relationship is a technical one that counselors need to master (1). We need to learn to adapt our clinical skills to a relationship which is somewhat different from the client-therapist one. When the teacher or general student personnel worker consults us, we need to learn how to keep focus on the specific issue he brings and simultaneously to attend to the dynamics of his being able to accept our help. We can hope that the psychological counselor can bring his special understanding of human behavior and development to the difficulties in understanding and dealing with specific students who are brought to him. But he must not overlook any subtle feelings of rivalry or other defensive feelings about having to rely on another which this act of consultation may provoke. After all, teachers and personnel workers are also expected to know something about students. The teacher's frustration at not being able to cope with his student may be assauged by demonstrating that the specialist can offer him no suggestions other than those he has already thought of, or that the novel suggestions offered are no more effective than his own ideas. The establishment of genuine collaboration, which can serve to diminish this status anxiety, requires that the consultant be reasonably free of status anxiety himself. Otherwise, he will augment the other's anxiety by his need to show that he has something to contribute; his attention and activities will be directed toward that goal instead of attending to what it is that keeps the teacher from coping successfully with his student, whether is comes from limitations in knowledge and technique or from special reactions that the particular student provokes in him. When the latter circumstance prevails, the most delicate and most perceptive clinical skills of understanding and action are required to be helpful without turning the consultation into the psychotherapeutic encounter that is not being sought.

This capacity to work with another around personal obstacles without setting up the conditions of psychotherapy is not only relevant to functioning as a consultant but applies even more to the direct influence that the psychological counselor can have on fostering identity formation. As should have been evident from the preceding discussion, self-confrontation and self-affirmation are central to the process of attaining a mature identity. For most students, interactions with their peers and with teachers and general personnel staff provide the necessary mediating experiences. In between this group and the smaller group of distinctly maldeveloped students, for whom special therapeutic treatment is indicated, is a large group who could achieve a workable degree of integration without further help but could be aided toward much fuller maturation through an encounter with a psychological counselor. To make such an encounter possible, the counselor must be willing to focus attention on specific issues such a student faces—his choice of curriculum and occupation, his difficulties in working well enough to satisfy his aspirations and his potential, and the problem of finding a satisfying niche in the student culture. The counselor must know how to work with this student so that the realistic issue is kept in focus while he is helped to confront those desires, anxieties, and other inner realities which make it difficult for him to cope with his problems. Remember that we are speaking of those who, without our help, would still reach a viable level of development. Our aim is that of all good education, to facilitate the individual's search for the full realization of his potentials, not just a viable one. It is through learning to exert effort and seeing how this will be patterned in an occupation that the student does the most work toward shaping and clarifying his identity. Elsewhere my associates and I (2) have argued that persons tend to gravitate to those occupations whose activities fit into their preferred ways of seeking gratification and of fending off anxiety. From this view, difficulties in making an occupational choice are seen as reflecting, for most students, trouble in coming to terms with themselves as part of identity formation. The student's struggle with the occupational issue becomes an important arena for working through such questions as how much of his parents' patterns shall be incorporated into his own, at what level of intimacy can he relate to others, and how acceptable to him are his ways of seeking pleasure.

Attention to the transitional nature of the problems that students face and to the goal of helping the student use the transitional period for constructive purposes has disclosed an area of help relatively neglected by me and most other counselors. The transition that the student goes through involves not only himself but his family. We have been well aware of his side of it, i.e., that he experiences ambivalent reactions of wishing to change his relation to his family and, simultaneously, of fearing loss of love and of not being able to face increased responsibility. Counselors have usually been aware that parents experience a corresponding ambivalence, but have not necessarily considered whether or how they might help parents cope with their part of the transformation. There is some truth in the position many counselors take that the basic problem for the student is an inner one and he is their client. Thus, when parents in their anxieties about facing changes in their relation to their child, anxieties reflecting both concerns for themselves and for the welfare of their son or daughter, approach counselors, the counselor is likely to respond solely in terms of the confidential nature of his relationship to the student. I suggest, however, that the ease with which a student negotiates this transitional period is, in part, influenced by his parents' freedom from anxiety and conflict about it. Thus, his client's welfare demands that the counselor take advantage of opportunities to aid his parents. For example, the issue of confidentiality itself, if approached in a manner other than that of self-righteous affirmation of the counselor's ethical responsibilities, can provide the parent with an opportunity to confront the fact that his son's maturation has brought both of them to the point where not all parts of his life will be shared with his parents and where he must begin to rely even more on himself than ever before. Parents often need help in seeing that these changes do not mean giving up all opportunities to be supporting and intimate in their relationships to their children, but do mean a change to a more mutual relationship of support and intimacy appropriate to adults. The student will live a more fulfilling future life to the degree that his parents have matured in this respect. It strikes me that colleges can fulfill an important social responsibility by including parents in their thoughts and plans for transitions, whether it is through orientation programs for new students, vocational counseling, or any other programs directed toward these ends.

This last topic of relationships to parents demands much more time than I have given it. But the time allotted to me has virtually disappeared. Fortunately, the program has planned for further discussion by a panel and in sub-groups. I hope that my ideas will become a part of your thought and that you can carry them forward as part of your professional identity, adding to them and modifying them in ways that make them your own.

REFERENCES

1. Bindman, A. J. "Mental Health Consultation." *Journal of Consulting Psychology*, 23:473-482 (1959).
2. Bordin, E. S., Nachmann, Barbara, and Segal, S. J. "An Articulated Framework for Vocational Development." *Journal of Counseling Psychology*, 10:107-118 (1963).
3. Erikson, E. H. "Identity and the Life Cycle." *Psychological Issues*, I:111 (No. 1, 1959).
4. Rosenthal, R., and Jacobson, Lenore. *Pygmalion in the Classroom*. New York: Holt, Rinehart, and Winston, 1968.

DISCUSSION

Panel

Chairman: WARREN S. WILLE, M.D., *Psychiatrist, Jackson, Michigan*
Dr. PHOEBE E. WILKINS, *MacMurray College*
Dr. HENRY F. GROMOLL, *Millikin University*
Dean CHARLES LEEDS, *Albion College*
Dr. WILLIAM L. KIRTNER, *Carleton College*

Dr. Wille: We should consider Erickson's description of "negative identity" in adolescence. Any aspect of a required role may bring on disdain and contempt. "Life seems to exist only where one is not, while decay and danger threaten wherever one happens to be." Adolescents, more than any others, can sense if you are phony. This applies to their peer groups, too! Let us re-emphasize Dr. Bordin's point, "We must respect the adolescent's maturity, but accept his immaturity." Kaplan defines "crisis" as a "temporary state in an individual's life which he cannot escape from and which he temporarily cannot deal with by using his existing repertoire of adaptive mechanisms." Adolescence is a period of considerable crisis. From the dynamic viewpoint, the individual may either break under too much stress *or* he may emerge from the stress stronger than before. Hence, stress can be a maturing experience. During stress there is an increased tendency to reach out for help from others. At times much help can be given by relatively untrained or inexperienced folk.

Dr. Wilkins: Why are student reactions to college stress different now than they were a few years ago? Are we hoist on our own petard? Have we taught a generation so much to rely on individualism that they now tell society to go hang? A recent study suggests "social activist" students are not in revolt against their parents but are actually carrying on their parents' ideals in liberalism and creativity. In our type of school we take students out of a permissive atmosphere and place them under a set of stringent rules and regulations. So perhaps we are not opening up the world to these students, but rather closing it in on them. This itself may set up alienation! The student paper on our campus recently called it an "ivory playpen." They questioned whether the college should stand between the student and the law, i.e., he should be responsible for the result of his actions. They are seeing further into their community relations and responsibility. The liberal arts colleges need to rethink some of their value systems or we may lose some of the best thinkers, the ones we really want to keep and develop.

Dr. Gromoll: I want to turn some of Bordin's thoughts to the identity problem of the counselor. He is no longer perceived as a mass vocational tester or as an isolated therapist dealing with students' intrapsychic roles in a social vacuum. Instead he may be viewed as a consultant, a trainer, and specialist in data retrieval. He thus may lead others to do the work traditionally done by the counselor. Smaller colleges will find the model of preventive community mental health less expensive and more efficient than the face-to-face method of meeting individual problems. A student coming for counseling with "a problem" is more prepared to talk about his pathology than to deal with his health. Thus we may help reinforce his pathology!

Dean Leeds: Some of us as personnel administrators must honestly admit at times that we may contribute to the alienation syndrome. Our challenge is to evaluate the effect our procedures and policies may have. If we can do our business in a way that shows we expect maturity, we will likely be more successful. We need to detect undue stress situations both inside as well as outside the classroom.

Dr. Kirtner: In my experience as a teacher and counselor I have not seen a very large sample of seriously upset students; most are moving smoothly toward conformity! Perhaps there should be a bit more of this alienation experience, since it may have value. To quote a character in Dr. Zhivago, "Do people really improve with age?" "Alienation," as often used in the vernacular, is a kind of dirty category, indicating that you are in a state of being wrong. Those who are getting this designation are often really the ones who are trying to clarify, redefine, reconstruct in a more honest, useful, meaningful arrangement the premises of human relationships. Most of these people (designated as "alienated") judge themselves by their own morals and ideals and hesitate to judge others quite as strongly. "Alienated" reactions should probably cause us to examine the college environment to see what induces these reactions! To me "alienation" is a term to help describe the set of conditions the person is either resolving, withdrawing from, rebelling against, refusing adherence to—a set of moral and ethical norms used by authorities to direct, control, and evaluate his behavior. And "identity" means a concept used to describe the set of moral and ethical norms and ideals held by the person whose identity is up for consideration. I disagree that college is a "last chance to be irresponsible." The college years are really a chance at a first fling at behavioral determination. It is one of the first periods, if not the only one, where life can move in directions not closely supervised by those with somewhat rigidly preconceived notions about what one is to like, to feel, to prize, and to head for. Free experimentation along these lines is usually found neither at home prior to college nor in work life and home responsibilities after college. College should offer a wider assortment of views and conditions to examine and evaluate. My question would be, what is the place of a program of content-oriented, fact-accretion oriented, idea-summation oriented education for a being who is teeming with problems about values, life, racism, or authoritarianism—all of them terribly relevant and significant? College is the one place in our society where it is possible to live out, love out, fight out some of these questions.

C. H. PATTERSON
University of Illinois

Some Problems and Proposals in College Counseling

● *Look* Magazine recently ran an article entitled "When College Students Crack Up" (18). Citing Dr. Dana Farnsworth (8), Director of the Harvard University Health Service, the article noted that, of every 10,000 college students, 1,000 have emotional problems severe enough to need professional help; 300 to 400 have feelings of depression deep enough to impair their efficiency; 100 to 200 will be apathetic and unable to organize themselves; twenty-five to fifty will be seriously affected by conflicts within the family; fifteen to twenty-five will need treatment in a mental hospital; five to twenty students will attempt suicide, and one to three will succeed. Multiply these figures by at least 600, since there are over 6,000,000 college students, and we have from 750,000 to a million college students affected by emotional disturbances, or from 10 to 15 per cent of the student population. Suicide, taking about 1,000 lives a year of the college population, ranks second as a cause of death for this group, and the rate is about 50 per cent higher for college students than for the population in general.

Hanfmann, et al. (11, p. 118), working in a small college (Brandeis University), suggests that about 5 per cent of college students are sufficiently disturbed to need psychiatric attention, but another 20 per cent, representing "cases of adolescent struggles and crises that are neither extreme or incapacitating" requires extensive or prolonged counseling.

These statistics do not include all the students who have educational and/or vocational problems, who have the more minor problems of adjusting to college or campus life, or to life and society in general. Probably more students drop out of college because of personal or emotional problems than because of academic failure. The total number of these students is uncounted. It has been estimated that as many as two-thirds, or four million, of our college students have psychological problems. To those who have been exposed to campus activities recently, this does not seem too high an estimate.

Not only the absolute numbers, but perhaps the proportion of college students with psychological problems will increase. There are two reasons for the possible increase in proportion as the college population increases. First is the increasing number of new students who in the past would not enter college because of their socio-cultural backgrounds. It is only reasonable to expect that the college experience and the college culture will lead to problems of a psychological nature for a large number of these students. A second reason is the apparent increase in psychological disturbance among youth in general. Perhaps "disturbance" is not a good term, since it implies abnormality, and the phenomena I have in mind are not all abnormal. What I am referring to is the increasing awareness and concern of youth about life and its problems, which is often accompanied by psychological or emotional reactions and conflicts, together with attempted solutions, some of which are not psychologically or socially useful. These solutions range from constructive participation, through revolt and resistance, to withdrawal and alienation from society.

I am concerned whether the constructive attempts are not being overshadowed by the nonconstructive attempts, if not in number at least by the attention which they are attracting. It is certainly a minority of students who are resorting to LSD and other drugs, to unconstructive revolt and resistance, or to withdrawal. But their number is large enough to produce a feeling that, because they are so numerous, they must be right. We are seeing ridiculous statements like that of Leonard Uhr (22), who wrote in *Psychology Today* that "the student ... who feels that LSD has given him a fresh view of the world, new understanding of himself, and a new warmth of compassion, is behaving much more in the great tradition of Western Civilization's search for the truth ... than is the more passive, well-adjusted individual who accepts the nontruths of official culture." One wonders whether, if these "feelings" were accompanied by a clearly psychotic state, the conclusion would be the same. And is it necessary or desirable to elevate one bad solution over another? In a broad sense all are attempts to withdraw and escape rather than to face the issues and make something out of one's life in what is admittedly not the best of all possible worlds. The protesters are doing nothing to improve the world, not even to make the contribution of developing themselves positively. The complaint that they have little power may be true, but they have no responsibility either. And until they demonstrate that they can assume responsibility, which begins with being responsible for one's self, it is ridiculous to turn society over to them. Their solutions are like that of the hashish user in the Arabic tale, who, with an alcoholic and an opium addict, found the gates of the city they were traveling to closed when they arrived after dark. The alcoholic wanted to pound on the gate to arouse someone. The opium addict suggested they sleep until morning. But the hashish user proposed that they slip in through the keyhole.

Whether psychological counseling is a remedy for this state of affairs—or whether there is any remedy except increasing age and experience—is a question. And if it could be a help, it is questionable whether those who most need help will seek it, though some do, according to our experience at the University of Illinois. Hanfmann, et al. (11, p. 51) notes that the most prominent "revolutionaries" of the school, the leaders in any fight against the administration, did not appear at the counseling center except when they experienced a severe breakdown. Perhaps there is something incompatible about being a revolutionary and a client in counseling or psychotherapy. In fact, counseling or psychotherapy could be, and unfortunately sometimes is, regarded as a method of control, a means of inducing conformity, of encouraging dependency, passivity, and acceptance of the status quo—that is, the fostering of adjustment to the world of adults.

This is why it is so important that college counseling services be divorced from administration. The current movement in counseling psychology to become involved in environmental modification is relevant here. Many counseling psychologists are suggesting that, since in their contacts with students they become aware of environmental conditions which are not conducive to optimum psychological health, they should intervene, through the administration, to modify or change these conditions. While it can be maintained that the counselor or counseling psychologist has some responsibility for creating a healthy psychological environment in schools and colleges as well as in society as a whole, the intervention in the school or college structure and program through the administration may influence the perception or image which students have of the counselor and the counseling service. The counseling service may be seen as an arm or agent of the administration, and students may doubt the confidentiality of their relationships with counselors. The intervention of counselors in the environment, and their relations to the administration, must be carefully considered.

At any rate, there appears to be an increasing awareness and concern in youth which I expect will lead more of them during their college careers to seek help in understanding themselves and in finding a meaning and a philosophy for their lives. The questions which we face are: Is this help going to be available? Should the college provide such help to students? How is the help to be made available if it is to be provided by the college? Who is to counsel the large numbers of students who need and want counseling?

It may seem unnecessary to raise the question of whether the college should provide counseling services for its students. The tremendous increase in student personnel services, which includes counseling, would seem to indicate that colleges have committed themselves to provide such services. But there is some question about the extent of this commitment. There are still many faculty members who feel that the function of an educational institution is the development of the mind or intellect, and that it has no responsibility or justification for becoming involved in other aspects of the student's life. It might be maintained that students who need assistance with personal or emotional problems should obtain it from other sources, either by going to private practitioners and paying for their services, or utilizing the services of community agencies or clinics. A narrow approach to education, which refuses to accept personality development as a concern of education, would support such a view. Of course, colleges have taken over many responsibilities for the personal lives of students, functioning in many respects *in loco parentis*. But there is evidence that this is changing. Stanton Millet, Dean of Students at the University of Illinois, in a report to the Board of

Trustees recently, stated that "it has become increasingly clear the day of an effective role for the university *in loco parentis* is dead." Are student personnel services and counseling, which are seen by some as "babying" or coddling students, or as encouraging dependence and lack of self-responsibility, to decline with the increasing independence of students and their assumption of more adult responsibilities?

This trend toward treating students more as adults than as children does not assure that the incidence of personal problems will decline. Adults also have problems. And the allowing of increased independence and responsibility might well lead to increased personal problems or need for assistance in developing independence and assuming responsibilities. If education is concerned with the development of the total individual, then it is concerned with his development as a person, as a member of social groups, and as a citizen in a society. The individual is a whole and cannot be separated into an intellect and a feeling, social being.

The recognition of this unity has led some to accept a limited view of personnel and counseling services. This view sees such services as justifiable for the purpose of enabling the student to function intellectually and academically up to his potential—to deliver the student to the classroom in a condition in which he can learn, as it used to be stated. But if education is broader than the development of the intellect, if it is concerned with the development of the person, then personal, social, and emotional development are justifiable goals in themselves, and are also of concern to an educational institution as part of the student's total education. Farnsworth (7, p. 8) states that "character education is as much a function of colleges and universities as the development of intellectual power."

At the present time it appears that adequate counseling services are not available for college students. The major public and private universities provide professional counseling services, but the majority of the over 2,200 colleges in the country have only inadequate if any counseling services available to their students. There are a number of reasons for this. One, which has already been mentioned, is lack of recognition of the need for counseling or of the obligation or responsibility of the college to meet the need. A second reason is the cost. Private colleges particularly may have problems here, although some of the smaller private colleges such as Brandeis have the most adequate services. Even the larger universities, with large counseling center staffs, are concerned about the cost of providing really adequate service, and as a result usually have limits on the number of counseling interviews a student may have, or discourage long-term counseling relationships. Bordin (2, p. 33) a number of years ago wrote that

> It is self-evident that society is neither willing nor able for economic reasons to devote more than a limited amount of its resources to this one kind of social service. A college or university might be willing to allot funds to make it possible for 20 per cent of its student body to receive an average of four or five counseling contacts in any given year. This would be a general allotment, and a sufficient budget would be found in only a minority of colleges and universities. It is unlikely that counseling services will expand far beyond this level of operation. Eight to ten contacts for the same proportion of students would probably be unrealistic and bring the budget for counseling staff into critical competition with that for teaching and, in some institutions, for research also. It seems unlikely that colleges or society in general will conclude that mental health services are so vital that other types of services must be sacrificed to them. Mental health practitioners themselves would hardly be willing to argue that they should be.

I am not able to tell whether colleges or society have changed in their attitudes towards the importance of mental health services. But it appears to me that four or five interviews for 20 per cent of the college population is not likely to make much of a dent in the problem, or adequately help very many students. It would seem particularly unwise for society to restrict services to college students, whose needs are greater than other groups, whose potentials for contributing to society are great, and who are more responsive to counseling than perhaps any other group. College youth are more open to change and have the characteristics which are conducive to change. They are going through a process of change, they are flexible, they are more open, natural, real, genuine, and spontaneous than most adults. Hanfmann, et al. (11, p. 118) note that although some students might "outgrow" their difficulties, they might also become a part of the large group of disturbed adults who constitute a problem and a burden to society. They note that "no significant personality changes can be expected to take place in the majority after the college years are over." It would appear that the investment in counseling of college students would be a good one for society, whatever the cost.

The alienation of many, the repression of one's being and experiencing, or the attempt to "play it cool" are defensive manifestations, retreats from the lack of direction or goals for change. The effective, adjusted, or fully functioning person (17, chap. 9), which is the goal of counseling, is open, genuine, or transparent, to use Jourard's term; as Jourard (14, p. 153) puts it, authenticity and self-disclosure mean "an end to 'playing it cool.'" He reports that applicants for services at a college psychological counseling center were lower disclosers of self than matched groups of students who had not sought counseling.

The increasing size and impersonality of colleges and universities are perhaps factors in the increasing alienation, loneliness, and isolation of the student which increases the need for counseling as an effort to establish some kind of a close relationship with someone. Social isolation, it has been noted (19) is the great common denominator in suicide, so prevalent, relatively, among college students. President Brewster of Yale is quoted by *Time* (20) as boasting that "Yale is still small enough that every student and faculty member is known intimately to someone who is known intimately to me." It may be questioned how long this will remain true, or how possible this will be in most colleges in the future, and, of course, whether this is sufficient to make counseling services unnecessary.

But there is another factor which affects the providing of adequate services, assuming that the desire and the money are available. This is the problem of manpower or the supply of professional personnel. Who is qualified to counsel students? Certainly we want qualified counselors, and we have progressed from the idea that any faculty member, if he had the time, could counsel any student. We have accepted counseling as a professional service. In some instances perhaps we have gone too far in establishing requirements. Some feel that counseling in the area of personal or emotional problems—or psychotherapy—must be performed only by or under the supervision of an M.D. or a psychiatrist. In a report of the Group for the Advancement of Psychiatry (10) the recommendation was made that, aside from the counseling done in deans' offices and by academic counselors, all counseling should be done by or under psychiatrists in student health services. As Farnsworth (7, p. 19), himself a psychiatrist, points out, this is unrealistic, since there are so few psychiatrists available. Most problems are not psychiatric in nature or degree, and do not require medical treatment, i.e., drugs or hospitalization. The identification of all counseling with psychiatry or medicine leads students to shun seeking help until their problems reach serious proportions, so that most do not get the counseling they need and the others often come too late to be helped.

In most colleges, however, counseling is seen as a function of psychologists, so that in most cases college counseling bureaus or centers are staffed entirely by psychologists. There is, however, too often an implicit if not an explicit restriction of services to educational and vocational problems, partly because of the reluctance to become involved in potentially long-term counseling or psychotherapy, but sometimes as the result of an artificial distinction between counseling and psychotherapy. An additional potential factor restricting counseling services, which seemed to be evident in a change of policy in one college counseling center recently, is the fear by the administration of unfavorable publicity when a student attempts or commits suicide or engages in other extreme behavior while being counseled. Of course, such behavior is possible while a student is being seen by a psychiatrist, but a medical degree seems to act as a source of immunity from suspicion of incompetence or blame, even though legally the psychiatrist and possibly the school may be sued for malpractice just as a psychologist or other professional person might be.

In general, however, there has been no question about psychologists engaging in counseling in the area of personal and emotional problems—or psychotherapy—provided they hold a doctorate. Currently, a doctorate in counseling or psychology is considered a requisite for counseling students at the college level. The shortage of such persons constitutes a severe restriction upon the offering of counseling services, particularly by smaller colleges which have difficulty in competing with the large universities for such persons.

Our discussion thus far indicates that there are a number of problems associated with providing counseling services which are adequate in nature and quantity for the large and increasing population of college students. I now wish to turn to a number of suggestions for resolving these problems.

1. Counseling services cannot be limited to educational problems or vocational problems, nor limited to a small, fixed number of interviews such as three or four or five. It should be obvious that the concerns and problems of present-day college students encompass the whole of life. Even though the student is ostensibly involved in full-time education and preparation for a vocation, these may not be his major areas of concern, either at a particular time or throughout his college career. The evidence from the college campuses is that other concerns overshadow them. The annual report of the Student Counseling Service at the University of Illinois indicates that of the approximately 5,000 students seen during the 1966-1967 year, only 10 per cent had problems which were largely or exclusively educational, and only 5 per cent had problems which were largely or exclusively vocational. Seventy-one per cent of the total group had problems which involved some admixture of significant personal problems, and 54 per cent of the students had problems which had educational, vocational, and personal aspects.

College counselors must be prepared to counsel students who present problems of a deep personal nature, involving identity, the meaning of life, concern over value conflicts within the self or between the self and society or parts of society. Counselors cannot focus upon a single, specific, practical or limited problem or accept a restricted or limited goal for counseling, since this compartmentalizes the person, isolating the specific problem from his life and person. Adherence to this narrow concept of counseling prevents the client from exploring himself and perhaps discovering or recognizing that what he thought was the problem isn't the real problem. The problem may be, or involve, the entire life of the student.

Counselors cannot be restricted administratively to dealing only with designated kinds of problems. The professional counselor must be prepared and willing, and permitted by the administration, to deal with any problem which the student presents or wants to discuss. If this is not the case, then the needs of students are not being met.

The counseling service should be concerned about the way it is perceived by students. I mentioned earlier the danger that its perception as an arm of the administration will keep students from using it. In the same way, its perception as being concerned only with educational or academic problems will keep students with other problems from coming in. There has been a tendency in most counseling services to foster, or at least not deny, this perception, in fear of becoming involved in long-term psychotherapy, or being flooded with more clients than could be handled. It is no doubt true that acceptance of students with other than simple or temporary educational-vocational problems would increase the number of interviews required by clients, probably considerably above the current average of two or three per client. But if the college is going to meet the needs of its students, this expansion of services must take place.

2. The second suggestion concerns the source of manpower, or the qualifications for counseling. As I noted earlier, the usual requirement for a position in a college counseling center is the doctorate. But it is obvious that there will never be enough people with the doctorate to meet the needs of two-year and four-year colleges and universities for counselors. What, then, is the solution?

The fact is that it does not require a doctorate to become a competent counselor or psychotherapist. In fact, much of doctoral training is either irrelevant or detrimental for the actual practice of counseling or psychotherapy. That the doctorate does not prepare one for counseling or psychotherapy is admitted in the claim of many that postdoctoral training is necessary for actual competence in practice. Many practicing clinical and counseling psychologists with the doctorate have complained about the inadequacies of their preparation.

As a matter of fact, most of the counseling being done in public and private agencies is done by persons without the doctorate. Although there is insistence that such counselors should be supervised by someone with a doctorate, the vast majority are not so supervised. There is no evidence that these counselors are not as helpful, or that they are any more harmful, than those with a doctorate. It is, of course, true that many of these counselors are inadequately prepared, and limited in their functioning and helpfulness by their lack of adequate preparation. But adequate preparation does not necessarily consist of meeting the requirements for the doctorate.

There is evidence that competent counselors can be produced with considerably less than doctoral preparation. I will refer to only a couple of the experiments demonstrating this. Several years ago the National Institute of Mental Health selected seven women, all at least college graduates, and gave them preparation in psychotherapy on a part-time basis (one-half to two-thirds time) for a two-year period. In terms of evaluations by four experienced therapists, and ratings by their clients, they were judged to be effective therapists (16). All the women scored above the average of candidates on the psychiatry subtest of the National Board of Medical Examiners examinations in psychiatry.

Carkhuff and Truax (3, 4, 21) have developed a program for the preparation of counselors, with no previous background or training, in 100 hours, concentrating upon the basic conditions of a facilitative human relationship. Comparison of these trainees on instruments developed to measure these conditions indicated that the program produced counselors who scored almost as high as a group of expert psychotherapists. These counselors were not, however, prepared to deal with vocational problems requiring knowledge and skill in using tests and educational-occupational information, nor were those trained in the N.I.M.H. program. Carkhuff concludes that counselors with such preparation "demonstrate counseling outcomes [measured by the evaluation of taped interviews] at least as constructive as their training supervisor or professional practitioners in general."

There is then no doubt that the doctorate in psychology or the M.D. are not required for the effective practice of counseling or psychotherapy. This should not be too surprising, since psychotherapy is essentially the providing of a good human relationship, and those with a doctorate do not have a monopoly on good human relationships. Some of us in counselor education have been convinced that we have been producing excellent counselors in our subdoctoral counselor education programs. The American Personnel and Guidance Association recommends two years of graduate preparation for professional counselors, and I believe that two years is sufficient to produce competent counselors capable of engaging in psychotherapy with the whole range of potential clients, including the severely emotionally disturbed. This result depends on the nature and quality of the program, however, and although there are a large number of institutions claiming to have two-year programs of counselor education, many, if not most, do not, in my opinion, produce highly competent counselors. But it can be done in two academic years if the program concentrates on the known essentials of counseling and psychotherapy.

Thus, there is a new potential source of supply for college counselors, and some are immediately available. Many other employers of counselors are competing for the products of these counselor education programs, but there is no reason why colleges cannot compete. Some of the students in these programs are interested in counseling in a college environment, but there have been few opportunities so far. I have talked with counseling center directors who have stated that they would be willing to employ well-trained counselors without the doctorate, but they have not done so to my knowledge. Meetings of directors of college counseling centers have recognized the inadequacy of the supply of doctorally trained counselors, and have discussed the employment of subdoctorally trained counselors, but there are few who have actually done so. There is certainly a problem in the selection of such staff members, since, as I have noted, the products of all counselor education programs are not adequately prepared for the general counseling function. But the time is coming when the employment of counselors without the doctorate will be accepted practice. Perhaps the smaller colleges have an opportunity to lead the way here.

The use of subdoctoral counselors (psychological counselors, rather than counseling psychologists) does not mean that there is no need or no place for the doctoral level counseling psychologist in the college counseling center. The counseling psychologist, with his broader preparation and his training in research, can function as the director of a center, or a senior staff member, with responsibility for supervision, consultation, and research as well as counseling some of the more seriously disturbed students.

3. A third major suggestion is the development of group counseling in colleges and universities. The use of group counseling is increasing. It has been emphasized that group counseling is not a substitute for individual counseling, and that it is not the preferred treatment for all students. The experience of a number of counseling services which have introduced group counseling has been that it has increased the demand for individual counseling, since almost all students who participate in a counseling group request, or are referred for, individual counseling. However, I question whether this

is necessary or desirable with most students if group counseling is skillfully conducted. There is evidence that group counseling is the treatment of choice for most adolescents. It would seem to be particularly appropriate for the kinds of problems many college students seem to have—problems of identity, alienation, isolation, problems of communication, etc. These students feel separated from society, from adults, and from each other. Thus group counseling would seem to be particularly appropriate for college students and for the suicidal potential of the isolated student. Many students spontaneously seek affiliations with others in some group. The popularity of fraternities is evidence of this, but fraternities offer only a selected or limited kind of togetherness. Dormitories are too large, though there are attempts to break them up into smaller living groups. But these are in effect accidental groups, and do not meet the needs of students for membership in a small, like-minded group.

Our society, of which the college or university is a representative segment in most basic respects, though misrepresentative in others, is a society in which, as sociologists have long pointed out, the small, face-to-face primary group is disappearing. The family is perhaps the only general primary group left. But the individual seems to need to be a member of some primary group, to be a member of a community in its basic sense. He needs a group in which he can feel safe, secure, where he can let his hair down, can be himself, can participate in close interpersonal relationships, can disclose his inner self to others, and not have to play a role or maintain a facade. That this need is general and basic to human beings seems to be indicated by the current rapid spread of small groups in all segments of our society, groups which go by various designations, such as T groups, sensitivity groups, basic encounter groups, marathon groups, as well as counseling groups.

The adolescent is no exception to this need for affiliation with others, indeed he may need and desire it even more than many adults who have developed defenses and shells which are difficult to break down.

Thus for many, if not most, of the problems of human beings, group counseling may be the method of choice, and thus not only a substitute for individual counseling but a preferred approach.

There are several other suggestions which may not be appropriate for most small schools or colleges which have no graduate schools with counselor education programs.

It was noted above that college counseling centers, particularly in the larger institutions, insist upon the doctorate for staff members. However, much, and in some cases most, of the actual counseling is performed by persons without the doctorate. These counselors are graduate students, usually at the doctoral level, enrolled in practicum courses in counseling or serving internships. This is an important source for counseling services for large institutions, available at relatively low cost, but it is a source which is, unfortunately, not available to the four-year college. It might be possible for some colleges to obtain such help from a nearby university which might assign and supervise its students for practicum experience. The fact that much of the counseling in the larger institutions is actually done by persons without the doctorate should encourage the employment of counselors without the doctorate in the smaller ones.

The possibility of developing proficiency in counseling in a brief, intensive training program suggests that it might be possible to increase the proficiency, and thus extend the services, of persons working as dormitory counselors. However, this is not likely to be a particularly useful solution because such persons usually continue on the job for only a year, and the investment in training would not be worth the cost of training. If graduate students preparing for counseling are available, these students could be employed as part-time dormitory counselors and provide more effective counseling services than the dormitory counselor who is not in a counselor education program. Students in counselor education programs could also provide counseling services in dormitories as part of their practicum experience. At the University of Illinois, privately operated residence halls are employing graduate students in counseling as part-time counselors. In addition, students in the counseling practicum are counseling in these residence halls.

Another suggestion which has been offered to help resolve the manpower problem is the use of faculty members as counselors. Farnsworth (8) suggests that faculty members will have to do most of the counseling in most colleges if it is to be done at all. This is unacceptable to me for a number of reasons. It is interesting that many psychiatrists, who would strongly resist even well trained persons engaging in anything called psychotherapy, encourage completely untrained persons to engage in counseling. Farnsworth does indicate that faculty members doing counseling should have available consultation with a competent psychotherapist. This solution is like the suggestion that teachers in our schools should do counseling when counselors are not available. But teachers and faculty members actually cannot become counselors. First, they are not prepared to counsel, and counseling does require some special preparation. Second, they do not have the time to do counseling, and it is unfair and beyond the expectation of the faculty member's contract to require him to give his time to counseling students. Third, even if faculty members were willing and able, in terms of competence, to counsel, there is a role conflict between teaching and counseling, and students in most cases would be unlikely to turn to faculty members for assistance on other than educational or academic problems.

In opposing the use of faculty members for counseling, I am not implying that college faculty should not develop closer personal relations with students on a nonacademic basis, participating in informal discussions, living in residence halls, and so forth. But this is not counseling.

There are a number of other problems and issues which we do not have time to go into, and which will no doubt be covered by other participants in this symposium. These include the one of reaching those students who need counseling when they need it, early enough, but not too early or before they are aware of any need. The evidence of research is that those who are not seriously disturbed objectively benefit most from counseling, although those with greater felt disturbance—that is, awareness of a problem or need—benefit more than those who do not feel disturbed. Students need to know of the availability of counseling services, yet they cannot be herded in for help. The desire for independence, to go it alone, is commendable, but help is often necessary, and counseling does not or should not foster dependence. A counseling service staffed by competent counselors, independent of the administration, known to respect confidences, accepted by faculty and staff, is basic to acceptance by students; but this may not be sufficient for maximum use of its services by students.

In summary, it may be stated that the need for counseling services may be greater among college students than among any other segment of our society. They are a selected group, but the nature of the selection insures that they are among the most sensitive to intrapersonal, interpersonal, and social-cultural discrepancies and conflicts. They are also, because of their age and background, more flexible and open to change, and thus more responsive to counseling. Their potential for leadership in society also makes them an important group. For all these reasons, then, it is desirable that adequate counseling services be provided. The cost to society may be relatively high, but the results will be well worth the cost.

The problems arising from the tremendous need and the shortage of professional personnel have been considered. It has been suggested that, to meet the varied needs of college students, college counseling services cannot concentrate upon or limit themselves to educational-vocational counseling. The personnel problem can be solved, at least in part, by the employment of counselors who have completed two years of graduate work in a good counselor education program. Finally, it has been suggested that the wave of the future will emphasize group counseling, which has a particular applicability for the kinds of problems of our current society, and the college student in that society.

REFERENCES

1. Blaine, G. B., Jr., and McArthur, C. C. (Eds.), *Emotional Problems of the Student*. New York: Appleton-Century-Crofts, 1961.
2. Bordin, E. S., *Psychological Counseling*. New York: Appleton-Century-Crofts, 1955.
3. Carkhuff, R. R., "Training and Practice in Counseling and Therapeutic Practices: Requiem or Reveille?" *Journal of Counseling Psychology*, 13:360-367 (1966).
4. Carkhuff, R. R., and Truax, C. B., "Lay Mental Health Counseling: The Effects of Lay Group Counseling," *Journal of Consulting Psychology*, 29:426-431 (1965).
5. Congdon, R. G., and Lothrop, W. W., *Survey of College Counseling Practices in the United States*. Durham, N.H.: University of New Hampshire Library (unpublished manuscript).
6. Escott, S. B., "Expanding College Counseling Services Through Graduate Student Utilization," *Counselor Educ. Superv.*, 7:36-41 (1967).

7. Farnsworth, D. L., *Mental Health in College and University*. Cambridge: Harvard University Press, 1957.
8. Farnsworth, D. L., *Psychiatry, Education, and the Young Adult*. Springfield, Ill.: Thomas, 1966.
9. Group for the Advancement of Psychiatry, *The Role of Psychiatrists in Colleges and Universities*. New York: Author, 1950.
10. Group for the Advancement of Psychiatry, Committee on the College Students, *Considerations on Personality Development in College Students*. New York: Author, 1955.
11. Hanfmann, Eugenia, et al., *Psychological Counseling in a Small College*. Cambridge: Schenkman, 1963.
12. Heath, D., *Explorations of Maturity: Studies of Mature and Immature College Men*. New York: Appleton-Century-Crofts, 1965.
13. Jacob, P. E., *Changing Values in College*. New York: Harper and Row, 1957.
14. Jourard, S. M., *The Transparent Self*. Princeton, N.J.: Van Nostrand, 1964.
15. Kaplan, L., *Mental Health and Human Relations in Education*. New York: Harper and Row, 1959.
16. Rioch, Margaret J., Elkes, Charmian, and Flint, A. A., *Pilot Project in Training Mental Health Counselors*. Washington, D.C.: U.S. Government Printing Office, 1965.
17. Rogers, C .R., "A Therapist's View of the Good Life: The Fully Functioning Person," in C. R. Rogers, *On Becoming a Person* (Boston: Houghton Mifflin, 1961), Chap. 9.
18. Shepard, J., "When College Students Crack Up," *Look*, 31(12):23-25 (1967).
19. Stengel, E., *Suicide and Attempted Suicide*. Baltimore: Penguin, 1965.
20. *Time Magazine*, 89(25):84 (1967).
21. Truax, C. B., and Carkhuff, R. R., *Toward Effective Counseling and Psychotherapy*. Chicago: Aldine, 1967.
22. Uhr, L., and Uhr, Elizabeth, "The Quiet Revolution," *Psychology Today*, 1(3):40-43 (1967).
23. Wedge, B. M. (Ed.), *Psychosocial Problems of College Men*. New Haven: Yale University Press, 1958.
24. Whitington, H. G., *Psychiatry on the College Campus*. International Universities Press, 1964.
25. Anonymous, "Suicide and Student Stress," *Moderator*, 5(4):8-15 (1966).

DISCUSSION

Discussion Leader: Dr. ROBERT S. BROWN, *Hope College*

Question: Can you elaborate on the possible role conflict between teaching and counseling?

Dr. Brown: I've been disturbed about the feeling these two are incompatible. The classroom experiences can be broadening and help one be more competent in his profession. And there are many good therapeutic classroom teachers operating (well) with much less than graduate training in counseling areas.

Dr. Patterson: I don't fully buy the concept, as some do, that "counseling is simply broader teaching." As I see it, facetiously, the greatest similarity between teaching and counseling is that they both use the "50-minute hour." There are similarities, but also differences. We hope teachers are therapeutic, but they are not therapists. The central difference is that teaching is certainly concerned with affect, but it is primarily cognitive in orientation. Counseling and therapy may be concerned with cognition, but they are primarily affect-oriented. It is a matter of emphasis. Psychotherapy *is* learning, but affective-learning is not the same as cognitive-learning.

Question: Dr. Patterson raised some questions about the training of the clinical Ph.D. and their competency as counselors. Part of this lies in the type of supervisor they may have had.

Dr. Patterson: To be a supervisor, or a consultant, one must know something about it. Most training programs emphasize the academic and cognitive, with less attention to real skills in counseling.

Question: Do we know about these skills?

Dr. Patterson: I think so. There has been a breakthrough here recently, particularly in the work of Traux and Carkhuff, as seen in their 1967 book (on the browsing table here at the Symposium). We no longer can say there is no evidence psychotherapy is effective. Eysenck's study is still quoted, but he never did a study. He just surveyed the research, and it is full of holes. Even he says that just because he couldn't discover any positive evidence of the effectiveness of counseling doesn't mean counseling is not effective. Most counseling research has been poorly done. One of the flaws is that clients have been lumped together and the "average" thus is based on some who improve and others who get worse. We used to feel a new counselor trainee couldn't really hurt anyone. A slip of the counselor's tongue might not hurt, even if the slip of a surgeon's knife would. We now have evidence slips of the tongue can hurt people. We now can identify counseling skills that help and those that hurt. This is well reviewed in the Traux and Carkhuff book.

Dr. Posin: In the Boston area a new Boston Student Center has just been set up by a group of psychiatrists, sociologists, psychologists, and social workers as a non-profit organization. They offer their services to the smaller educational institutions of the area who have inadequate staff of their own. They will deal with administrative staff, consult with personnel people, or do therapy with individual students. This is a device to increase resources. Let me add that as a psychiatrist the more I see the counseling or therapy relationship, the more complicated I realize it is. Your proposal of a new type of trainee is basically a good idea. But the good therapist must be fully aware of the potency of the relationship. I was appalled at the N.I.M.H. program of training housewives as therapists; I would fear they really couldn't be aware of the complexity they were dealing with.

Dr. Brown: I don't feel it is simple and hope I didn't waste my seven years in Ph.D. preparation. I'm skeptical, too, about "100-hour wonders." I don't see them as being able to function independently. They certainly need supervision and to have their clients selected for them. The basic human relationships may be simple, but they are not simple to implement! But if in training we concentrate on the essentials, and eliminate non-essentials, we can get training more relevant to our functions in counseling. We don't want to be like the college senior who said, "My father didn't get enough out of my college education!"

Question: At times it is very convenient for counselors to hide behind the veil of "confidentiality" when they see pathology in the organizations they represent, i.e., creating problems in students and not doing anything about it (in the whole) but just working with the individual students. Aren't we responsible for doing something about our institution if it puts unnecessary stress on the students?

Dr. Brown: I agree, but it needs to be done carefully. We must not destroy our relationship (confidentiality) with the student who is the real source of our knowledge of the stress factors.

Question: Aren't we, as professionals, better equipped to recognize and handle this? Our faculty is now letting us bring out and discuss some of the situations we used to know but would hide. We let students bring their points of view to the faculty and they find it refreshing.

Question: I'd like to return to the issue of training, where there is still some inconsistency in our comments. We have been arguing for shorter training periods in counseling, and, on the other hand, arguing this won't help meet the real complexities in therapy. Are we saying the shorter-trained person is all we should have on the smaller college campus? I think the schools represented here have more well-trained counselors, with their Ph.D.'s doing counseling than a lot of major universities. The better small schools are in a good competitive position in attracting well-trained counselors, because they want to be engaged in active counseling and therapy (and teaching) rather than bogged down in the remote research operations that go on in the larger universities.

Dr. Patterson: I'm taking the middle position, i.e., the "100-hours" is not enough, but the Ph.D. is not necessary. Two years is adequate, at least in our program, without adding two more years for the doctorate. You can do it in less than "seven years" if you concentrate on the fundamentals, which we now begin to know. The Ph.D. is a research degree, not training for therapy.

Question: What does your two-year program consist of?

Dr. Patterson: First year is full time academic background—counseling theory, measurement, testing, personality, plus some laboratory experience. Third semester is practicum, as staff members in the counseling center at an Air Force base, fifteen miles away, at least three half-days per week. There is supervision (later) in which every case is discussed, but they have basic responsibility. There are also staff meetings with the neuro-psychiatrists at the base. The clients range from pre-school children to adults with marital problems. The fourth semester is an internship in an off-campus agency. Our program gives didactic training and background in the first year, which then is followed by practicum. Many schools are putting them in practicum immediately, in their first year, and this can be dangerous.

Question: We talk some of doing "social engineering" on our campuses. Should we conceive of our college community as a "big Skinner box?" What role should the counselor play in feed-back from students?

Dr. Patterson: The counselor, along with others, does have responsibility for changing institutions. But people must change through people; it is not mechanical. However, counselors must see there is difficulty in being perceived as an agent of the institution, rather than as agent for the student.

Dr. Norris: I want to comment about the role of the counselor and the teacher. We are told the stepped-up academic program now creates tension and therefore generates emotional problems. Thinking back, the best teacher I ever had was the toughest, one who put on an awful lot of pressure. Pressure can be good, it may initiate action, shake us out of our heads. So where are we on this question?

Dr. Brown: Pressure is good for some people, but devastating to others. A good distinction is that there is difference between a challenge and a threat. If you challenge, he responds positively; to threat, he responds negatively. The line between the two varies for different individuals.

Dr. Norris: Then there is no real answer to educational administrators about whether tightening up academic pressure is good or bad?

Dr. Brown: You can set some minimum standards, and if people can't conform to those standards then this is not the place for them.

Voice from the Rear: Perhaps Mr. Chips is no longer the ideal. Maybe he never was!

LESTER A. KIRKENDALL
Oregon State University

An Emerging Morality and the College Counselor

● Newspapers and magazines are filled with discussions about the "new morality." The mass media are much preoccupied with the subject. But in spite of this widespread interest, a great diversity of opinion still exists about what constitutes the new morality.

Some say that it is simply the old immorality in a new garb. Others feel sure that we are moving into a period in which we will develop concepts of morality more adequately suited to man and his needs.

To most casual thinkers the new morality is in some way involved with sex, and for them the linkage is simple enough. One of my students put it succinctly when I asked a class for their understanding of the new morality. He said, "It means more and freer sex." The determinent in whether there is a new morality seems to be simply the question of whether incidence figures for non-marital intercourse are changing. If incidence figures are rising immorality is "rampant"; if they are not rising morality is at least holding its own.

This view was implicit in a widely disseminated press release which appeared in early June, 1967. The story carried such headlines as "College Girls Still Moral As Ever" or "Professor Declares Morality Not Declining." The stories featured an article written by Dr. Seymour Halleck, professor of psychiatry at the University of Wisconsin, and published in the *Journal of the American Medical Association*. (1) I quote excerpts from the news report.

> The common impression that sexual morality is vanishing from American college campuses just isn't so. Dr. Halleck says surveys indicate "no appreciable increase" since 1910 in the proportion of girls having inter-

course before marriage. "... the physical state of virginity still seems to be the norm," he reports.

The lack of awareness that sexual morality involved anything beyond renunciation or participation in intercourse or that moral issues extended beyond sexuality is typical of our culture.

The phrase "the new morality," as it is commonly used, has a quality about it which leaves me far from enthusiastic in accepting it as a term to designate a viable and dynamic concept. The expression has a static feeling about it. It implies that we have already arrived at some concensus or condition of stability in our opinions about morals, that there is something which can really be called "the new morality." Yet clearly there is nothing that definite or so precise. What has brought about the present public discussion is that we are finding the old forms—the traditional morality—inadequate and irrelevant in today's world. Furthermore, we are clearly uncertain as to what all this collapse means, what we should be thinking, or even as to what constitutes a desirable morality.

Frankly I do not see that we have a new morality. However, the outlines of what might be a genuinely new morality may possibly be emerging now. We are hopefully in the process of developing a different approach to moral thinking—an approach which will have much significance for counselors, and for everyone working with people and/or everyone concerned with human relationships.

In order to make clear what is happening and what is needed, it would be helpful to contrast features of the traditional morality with the emerging morality—for *emerging morality* is the term I prefer to use.

Certain features of the traditional morality which have made it unworkable and brought it into a state of disrepute should be noted.

First, the traditional morality has presumed that morality was contained within a pattern of permitted or denied acts. The morality of a person was determined by the extent to which he adhered to or deviated from this behavior code. This was assumed in the news release I have just quoted.

Centering around acts as it does, the traditional moral code has in actuality frozen us into patterns of behavior the meanings of which have greatly changed. Even while these changes have been occurring, moral thinking has remained unchanged and has even staunchly resisted change. The problems which arise as a result reflect a paralyzing hiatus between wistful attachment to what was and actuality. This in a large measure results from the impact of science. Scientific developments in medicine and technology have changed ways of looking at and thinking about life and death itself.

The separation of reproductive outcomes from sexual functioning is one of the developments which is requiring new thinking about sexuality. Intercourse can now be engaged in with the practical certainty that pregnancy can be prevented. Whether a couple should have children becomes a matter of choice and conscious decision. Effective contraceptives now make it possible to experience sexuality in the service of purposes which are completely apart from reproduction. Thus sex may be regarded as and participated in strictly as a communicative experience. The use of sex for pleasure-recreational outcomes becomes perfectly possible, and from a rational and humanistic point of view quite permissible.

But now the lessened need to use sex for procreative purposes is changing our whole concept of the purpose and character of sex acts, and consequently of sexual morality. Sex standards as they originally evolved reflected the need for tying sexual activity to procreative outcomes. Any use of sex which did not contribute to reproduction was threatening, since if the species was to survive, reproduction and sexual activity needed to be linked closely. Acts which did not contribute to procreation or could not result in reproduction became tabooed, immoral acts. This need for sex to serve reproductive outcomes helped give rise to the moral restrictions against homosexuality, masturbation, and the use of contraceptives.

A loud, clear echo of this view is heard in the statement attributed to Pope Paul VI in an interview printed in a recent issue of *McCall's* magazine. (2) Referring to contraception, the Pope is quoted as having said that it (along with nuclear armament) is an invention "hostile to life and directly contrary to the primordial precept of Genesis: 'Increase and multiply.'" The interdiction of the Catholic church against birth control, except as abstention from intercourse is the method used, is regarded by Pope Paul as "a law of love, a law which preserves and increases true love, in protecting it from illusions and deviations." Apparently the Pope still sees no clear and proper use for sexuality except as it is used in the service of procreation.

Just as the meaning of reproduction and the significance of sexuality has changed, so has the meaning and significance of dying. Advances in the field of medical technology have made it possible to prolong life considerably beyond the time when under ordinary circumstances the individual would have died. It is possible to keep the respiratory and cardiac systems operating long past the time when the individual can have any hopes of ever again becoming a functioning individual. The consequence is that there is now a moral debate over the undue prolongation of life.

During the early part of 1966, I was visiting professor at the University of Kansas Medical Center. Here I came in contact with discussion groups in which this issue was being considered. At one point one of the doctors remarked that "we now need a new definition of death." This was startling, for I had thought death was an easily distinguishable occurrence. But apparently medical and technical developments have changed the meaning of death.

A second feature involving our traditional moral code is that it has been too exclusively associated with and considered an aspect of traditional religion. Religious leaders were considered *ipso facto* moral authorities. As a consequence, traditional thinking about morality has had serious limitations and weaknesses which are now making it irrelevant. For one, morality as an acts-accepting—acts-rejecting code of behavior has been assumed to rest upon unchanging, infallible supernatural authority. This is the assumption implicit in an article which appeared in a newspaper in July, 1967. The story had to do with "the new morality."

> There is much talk in today's religious circles about a "new morality." The term indicates that there is a different set of rules for life today than there was ten or fifty or two thousand years ago.
> Morality is morality, timeless and unchangeable. If it is moral it is neither new or old. It is just moral. . . . The source of true morality is God and He never changes.

This reliance on a transcendent, immutable, unvarying authority is being rejected by more and more people, even very religious ones. In our science-oriented society we have come to rely increasingly upon the processes of scientific inquiry, empirical authority, and tested hypotheses and demonstrated results in making decisions. We depend upon weighing and evaluating possible outcomes and upon reaffirmed conclusion for our authoritative sources.

Another weakness of traditional morality is that moral evaluations have typically been used judgmentally and punatively. Moral judgments, once made, have then been used to isolate those who transgressed or violated the code. Quoting again from the same newspaper source as before:

> This man who is guilty of [sexual] sin is living a life of lust as the devil would have him live.
> The church is to take formal action and turn him out of the church. Members should separate themselves from the sinning one. They do not have the power or the authority to deal with the man's soul. That is in the hands of God. They do have the authority to separate a sinner from fellowship thus bringing conviction so his spiritual problem can be brought to light for the Lord to deal with him.
> Immorality is not approved by God. There is no new morality as far as He and His Word is concerned. The church must not allow this kind of thing to continue in its midst. . . .

Moral living is too often made to seem glum, dour, and joyless. As one of my students said, "I should think if one always lived morally, it would be a pretty dull life." Semantically, a number of our traditional expressions reflect the point of view that to be evil is very easy and attractive, to do right is very difficult. According to this view, righteous living is possible for only a few. Evangelical religionists say of righteous living: "many are called, but few are chosen," and those who are are the "elect." Reference is made to the "straight and narrow path" trod by the elect, and the "primrose path to hell" which "lures the weak." Another common expression is that those who seek "salvation" must "fight their way through." Is it any wonder the student had the attitude he did about the glumness of the moral life?

Still a third weakness of traditional morality is that it has been centered on sex so predominantly and exclusively that other issues of great moral significance have been overlooked. Furthermore, behavior which violated the sexual code has been made to seem more evil than any other. The same article from which I have been quoting commented as follows: "The seriousness of fornication was such that Paul said even the unsaved population was more moral . . ."

What I am protesting are the processes of rigidification and institutionalization which are found in various of the fields of human relations. In government, old forms, patterns, and ways of thinking defeat efforts to right wrongs, to correct injustices, and to move to a more effectively functioning governmental structure. In the behavioral science field some of the great thinkers have been made into transcendent authorities not to be questioned or challenged. Insightful thinkers such as Freud, Marx, Lenin, and others have been turned into authorities by their apostles, and their pronouncements have been given an air of finality which has in some ways and for some persons made the behavioral sciences as rigid as any of our other institutions.

Within segments of organized religion itself this punitive, judgmental approach is being seriously weakened. Basically this need for a more flexible approach to moral considerations is what is today rocking the Catholic church. Leaders in the Protestant church and other religions as well have recognized the importance of moving to a more flexible basis.

The situation ethicists have made a clear break with the rigid, legalistic approach to moral considerations. This movement has gained much prominence in the last few years. Bishop John T. Robinson of England, author of *Honest to God* (3), and Rev. Joseph B. Fletcher of Boston, author of *Situation Ethics* (4) are the best-known of the situation ethicists.

These two and other theologians wish to break away from legalistic and rigid interpretations of rules and customary patterns of behavior. They are protesting behavioral practices which have become institutionalized to the point of being ends in themselves. Basically they are concerned with making the principle of loving care for others the foundation for moral decisions. This concern is, of course, not exactly new. Jesus protested the legalistic interpretation of the meaning of the Sabbath, and many before and since have fought the same legalism.

The situation ethicists strike a warm chord of sympathy in me. Rather than regarding myself within this group, however, I prefer to emphasize the need for developing responsible, meaningful interpersonal relationships. This is the goal we should be seeking as we make human relations decisions—decisions about the use of our sexuality, our intellect, our physical strength, our speech, and any other of our capacities or potentialities. The creation of meaningful interpersonal relationships is the criterion against which we need to check our decisions and our results.

As we choose alternatives concerning behavior and crystallize our ethical viewpoints, the moral decision will be the one which works toward the creation of trust, confidence, integrity, and outreach in both primary and secondary relationships, now and in the future. Acts which create distrust, suspicion, and misunderstanding, which build barriers and destroy integrity, are immoral. And this is, of course, another way of stating "the law of loving care."

The interpersonal relationship approach seems to me to provide an element of specificity and a certain clarity which is lacking in the "situational ethics" discussions. Many persons who are in essential agreement with the situational ethicist seem to have concluded that in this approach every situation requiring a decision presents a wholly new set of circumstances. As a result they find themselves immobilized by the need to analyze each human relations situation from scratch. They are unsure in their decision-making about what factors need to be taken into account. They are not clear as to the nature of love, or what it requires of them. So while they are tired of a legalistic interpretation of regulations imposed by fiat, they are lost when it comes to knowing how to proceed within the broad, diffusely-defined framework of the situation ethicist.

The impact of premarital intercourse upon interpersonal relationships, I found, was susceptible to study and analysis (5) once the term interpersonal relationship had been defined. While I make no brief for the relationship components I used as being inclusive or final, I did isolate as components the character of communication, the nature of motivations, and the readiness of individuals to assume responsibility. These components varied in their form of expression and meaning for the relationship according to the degree and the mutuality of the affectional involvement felt by the partners. By examining the various combinations of these components in relation to the degree and mutuality of affectional involvement, and through the insights derived from the analysis of other data obtained in the study, I have been able to help individuals evaluate more realistically the extent to which their sexual relations are expressions of love, hostility, or satisfaction of personal ego.

Utilizing the characteristics of an interpersonal relationship and understanding the processes involved in being meaningfully related, there is no need for starting afresh with every situation. The relationship components are present in the various situations. With experience and developing insight one can anticipate what impact they will have upon the relationship and what outcomes are likely. Some guiding "generalizations" can be developed, not with absolute certainty but with enough assurance to make sense. One can never be sure of a generalization in any situation, but, for example, the chances are high enough that a disastrous accident will occur if one drives 125 miles an hour in crowded traffic on a slippery pavement that I support the regulation which forbids it.*

This way of thinking should be familiar to anyone versed in the behavioral sciences. It has great significance, for I believe the greatest help in arriving at a more meaningful concept of morality is found in the approach being made by some of the leaders in the behavioral sciences. Here we have a number of scholars concerned with understanding what people are like, how they come to be what they are, and what they may become. These scientists are concerned with what goes on in schools, homes, and churches; they are interested in the development of persons whom we would appreciate as neighbors, persons with whom everyone could live securely and with satisfaction. The kind of people these leaders envision are the kind needed in a humane, compassionate society.

Without going into detail about any of these scientists, I will mention some of them. I know, too, that I will have omitted some who fully merit inclusion, and for this I apologize. We have Fromm talking about the productive man; Rogers, the fully functioning person—the person open to all his experiences; Maslow, the self-actualizing person; Jourard, the authentic being who is able to disclose himself; Horney, the real self; Huxley, the fulfilled person; Glasser, the responsible person; Saul and Jahoda, the mature person; and Szasz, the autonomous person. Mower discusses the person of

---

*The preceding three paragraphs are adapted from my article, "Sex Revolution—Myth or Actuality?" *Religious Education*, 61(6), 411-18, November-December, 1966.

integrity, Frick and Nelson Foote talk about persons who are competent in their interpersonal relationships. Montagu emphasizes the importance of love and the role of the co-operative person in human relations, just as in the field of theology, Fletcher and Robinson talk about the caring, loving person. The people these authorities would like to see as the product of their efforts are described by the terms they have used, e.g., the productive person, the responsible person.

This point of view is apparently what Girvetz, et al. (6) had in mind when they wrote,

> Whether it be "self-actualization," "positive freedom," "relief from tension and anxiety," "dynamism," "creative interchange," "human dignity," "total personality," or something else (all of them inadequately and almost caricaturishly denoted in a bare list like this and even by the naked labels themselves), the source of values appears to lie in an integrated experience where problems do not fester but are resolved.

This discussion will doubtless impress some as being full of piety and good-will and lacking in substance. Actually it is based upon a very important assumption supported by scientific evidence which is being accepted more and more widely. This is the assumption that man is by nature a social animal. His nature, in fact his very survival, demands satisfying associations in which he can feel secure and accepted and in which he can reveal himself. It is in his close associations with others that he finds his deepest satisfactions and his profoundest miseries, and through which he develops from a biological organism into a humane, zestful human being. If man is by nature a social creature, then his conduct needs to be directed toward helping in the maximum development of his social capacities.

Girvetz, et al. makes the same point. They write:

> ... when a Karl Menninger, among others, demonstrates in detail the relation of mental health to the outgoing activities of what he does not hesitate to call "love," and the contrary pathological tendencies involved in withdrawal and cruelty, it can be argued that experimental and verifiable knowledge about man and his relationships to others is helping in some cases to justify, and elsewhere even to establish, norms of conduct....

> ... man must live if he is to live well, but until he lives well—developing his curiosity, widening his horizons, exploiting his capacities for intellectual growth, keeping sharp and alert his sensitivity to beauty, cherishing his

communion with others—he still has not satisfied his most characteristic wants. Professor A. H. Maslow, summarizing the "new knowledge" about values (7), remarks that among (celebrated) scientists there is almost unanimity on the imperative of "decentering" for a healthy and desirable life. This refers to the seeking and achieving of affection, warmth, union with others in various ways—in general, the socializing of man without which he becomes truncated and impoverished. Such a recommendation is not simply hortatory in the sense that man is being urged to consider his fellow men with charity; the social factor is being singled out as a main contribution to a sound and rich life.

If this view of man and his morals were to be accepted and implemented it would require pronounced changes in ways of thinking. I believe it would mark the end of discussions about morals and morality. In the not-too-distant-future, perhaps discussions of morality in the traditional sense will seem as outdated as discussions of witchcraft and sorcery. Much more meaning can be derived and much more help given by discussing how we can move positively toward the realization of that which is best in our human potential. So far as I am concerned, I would like to dispense with discussions of morals and morality. I would prefer to talk about how families, schools, churches, and civic institutions can build autonomous, fully-functioning, loving persons, and depend upon this to take care of the moral issue.

Most counselors are already deeply involved in moral issues and are practicing moralists, if this point of view is accepted. Why do I say this? How would a counselor regard his approach and his results if he were to implement this way of thinking in his professional work?

First, *the counselor would be concerned with the growth and fulfillment of all persons within the context of loving, caring relationships*. A major objective would be the extension of such relationship ultimately to include more and more persons. He would be interested in furthering the outreach of his clients, with widening their world and with making it a place in which it is good to live. These objectives seem in harmony with the objectives of the behavioral scientists just mentioned. If accepted by the counselor they certainly result in his being actively concerned with value-laden decisions. In this sense, then, he becomes a moralist.

Second, *the counselor would be concerned with how to help*

his clients grow, develop, and move toward the realization of their personal and social potentialities. He would be interested in helping them become whole, fulfilled, integrated persons. This will require him to focus very heavily upon relationships, since it is through relationships that people realize their social potentialities. The counseling focus is commonly upon the individual and his problems, his defeats and frustrations, and attention should be given here. But improvement really comes, and significant (and moral) behavioral changes occur as the client experiences the satisfaction of deep and meaningful relationships. It is in his relationships that an individual experiences his keenest agonies. The task of the counselor is to help him in establishing satisfying ones.

In pursuit of this objective I find that I have focused with increasing intensity upon relationship considerations. Rather than simply listening to an individual discuss a disturbing relationship (and one which he has had a share in disrupting) with the hope that he will gain insight, I often raise the issue of how to improve or restore relationships.

This is a simple enough approach at the primary, dyadic level. I have worked with many a student in thinking of ways in which he could overcome his own resistances to efforts directed toward improving relationships with his parents. I have on occasion become considerably more directive than some of the theoretical formulations would suggest as desirable. For example, a premaritally-pregnant young couple came to inquire about legal requirements for marriage in different states. Their intention was to go to a state where they could fib about their age, get married quickly, and then confront their parents with an accomplished fact. Their agitation and panic was obvious; they could face their parents only if they had corrected their sexual misdoing by marriage. Nevertheless they hoped ultimately for good relationships with the parents. Under the circumstances I insisted vigorously that the couple do nothing until they became much calmer. I also argued that my best insights led me to feel that if they did want the support and understanding of their parents they were proceeding in exactly the wrong direction. They were likely to make relationships worse rather than better. Ultimately they decided to follow my suggestion and get in touch with their parents before marriage rather than after. In this instance the procedure adopted did make for better relationships all around.

In such a situation, the way in which relationships and relating are involved is quite obvious. In other counseling situations the connection may be less obvious.

On a number of occasions I have dealt with males who have been reacting to strong feelings of jealousy toward dating partners. On occasion these feelings are so extreme as to make it almost impossible for them to date without so possessively engulfing their partners that relationships break. In the case of an individual who reacts this way it is not uncommon to find he has a history of working in deceptive, dishonest, double-standard relationships with girls. After a period of success in such relationships he loses respect for the girls because they are gullible, lacking in shrewdness and judgment. His experience convinces him that most males approach women in this way and are successful in getting what they want. One thing he is sure of is that all women succumb to such approaches. The result is that too little respect is left to maintain the relationship. His method of insuring his own relationship with a girl for whom he cares against such disaster is to avoid scrupulously his typical double-standard behavior. He also jealously isolates his girl friend from the approaches of other males. And the stage is thus all set for trouble.

In a number of such instances, following the relationship approach which I have been explaining, I have encouraged the jealous individual to return to the girls of whom he had earlier taken advantage, and rectify to the extent possible the exploitation which had occurred. The objective was to right, insofar as possible, the wrongs which had been done, and to help both parties in the restoration of a healthy self-respect. The results have been strikingly good. One individual with whom I worked was quite resistant to my suggestion that he follow this procedure. After much discussion he accepted the idea. Then followed a long period of procrastination and vacillation. Finally he did embark upon his program of apologizing for the exploitations in which he had engaged. He returned later to discuss his feelings about what had been accomplished. One of his significant comments was, "I walked away from that experience [of talking through his exploitative conduct with a particular girl] feeling like a man." At the same time he had been able to relax

AN EMERGING MORALITY 57

in his relationships with his girl friend, and feelings of jealousy were lessening.

Over the past four years I have worked with a young man whom I knew first as a seventeen-year-old boy. He was in trouble emotionally, and had experienced a rupture within his family which led to his being asked by his father to leave home. He was sexually promiscuous and was otherwise in trouble with the juvenile authorities. In working with him I did not concern myself with behavior patterns except as I judged changes would enable him to be more responsible, realistic, and open in his relationships. Thus I was concerned with the sexual relationships in which he was engaging not because they were sexual relationships, but because they were irresponsible, deceptive, and essentially exploitative. Decisions about the behavior patterns he would follow were his, though I sought ways to emphasize the goal of responsible behavior which embodied integrity and openness. I feel that this approach has borne fruit.

While there are still some problems, I am today dealing with a much more mature, responsible young man. He is trying to order his associations (to live morally, if you will) in terms of the demands which loving, caring relationships make on people. His intention has been to make openness, honesty, and responsibility in relationships the cornerstones of his philosophy.

Recently he wrote a paper in which he commented upon his effort to redirect his life. He has not renounced premarital intercourse (which would be the prime concern of some) within the context of caring relationships, but he has moved away from the casual, promiscuous relationships which were exclusively his pattern when I first knew him. The amount of sexual participation has clearly diminished, and his willingness and ability to assume responsibility in those relationships he does experience has clearly increased. He has restored his ties with his own family and through honesty and candor has removed many of the contradictions and conflicts which plagued him at seventeen.

In his paper he discussed his changing attitudes toward relationships and toward sex, the altered character of his sexual patterns, and the restoration of good relationships with his own family (which have been maintained now for about two years). His relationships with a number of other persons have improved also. I quote:

> It has been a revelation to find that being open when dealing with others caused others to be open to me in return. My capacity for being free and open with others has been increased. I have come to see girls as persons rather than objects through which I could achieve masculine status. All this has had a tremendous impact on my sexual relationships. I no longer find intercourse merely a physical pleasure. Because I have been able really to know my partner as a human being who feels love, hate, pain, frustration, warmth and closeness, the physical sensation of merely embracing her is exhilarating. My relationships are now usually satisfying enough to maintain themselves without intercourse, but if and when intercourse does occur, it adds to and enhances the relationship instead of dominating it.
>
> I have become better able to integrate sex into relationships as an intrinsic part, but it is not nearly as crucial a part as I formally thought it was. My satisfaction stems now from experiencing the love, warmth, and closeness that I have learned is within others and also within myself. I also know this closeness can be expressed in ways other than sexual. I have found that touching is another wonderful form of communication. This is another discovery that has changed my attitude toward sex and love.*

I believe that with this individual there is now a more meaningful morality even in conventional terms than previously existed, and that rather than being a dour and walling-in experience it has been a releasing and fulfilling one. For example, he also wrote this:

> It took me a great deal of time to establish the cherished relationships I now have, and maintaining and building them is a continuing process. My relationship with my father is wonderful, and we are still furthering it. Every time we come together we discover new things about each other, some good, others not so good. But the more we discover about each other, the closer we become. Even as I write this and reflect on our relationship, I feel a tremendous excitement.

Living in meaningful relationships is a satisfying experience, and by virtue of this, responsible, outreaching, loving behavior, while exacting, becomes meaningful and increasingly possible.

Third, *the counselor will approach his clients as autonomous, decision-making persons who have potentialities and wish to realize them*. He will not, however, try to provide them with answers. Instead he will be concerned with the decision-making process and

---

*McDermott, Robert J., "Realities of the Young." Unpublished manuscript. Quoted by permission.

with helping the individual make decisions which leave both him and those with whom he is associated with a sense of being meaningfully related.

Being interested in decision-making, the counselor will be concerned with increasing the number of alternatives and widening the range of choices within the framework of loving, caring, responsible conduct. Instead of narrowing the choices as the traditional morality does, the emerging morality will require him to expand and examine the possibilities which can be found within this framework. He will talk, not in terms of didactic certainty, but in terms of what he knows about the possible outcomes associated with the different alternatives. He will talk in terms of probabilities and possibilities, and interpret existing knowledge and research findings in terms of potential choices. He will take problems like interracial marriage, divorce, childbearing patterns, the daily experiences of human interaction and subject them to analysis based upon pertinent knowledge and the meaningful experiences of human beings. Possible ways of dealing with drug usage or varying sexual standards would be discussed and decided upon, evaluated and re-evaluated in terms of what is known and what is learned from human experience.

Of course this widening process is proceeding without the benefit of counselors. For example, in the past I have often discussed with unmarried individuals or with couples, decisions they are facing about how they will handle their sexuality within the dating relationship. Some are still making decisions at a relatively elementary level. They are puzzling over such questions as, "Is any physical expression between couples which has sexual arousal in it, satisfactory for us?" "How far shall we go with petting?"

The last several years, however, the persons or couples with whom I work have raised decision-making questions at a new level of sophistication. They are commonly, I believe, accepting sexual expression of some kind as a foregone conclusion. Their questions are rather at what level shall sexual expression occur? "Should, or can, it be confined to petting?" "What are the advantages or disadvantages of sex play to climax?"

More broadly and more frequently, I find them asking about and experimenting with various forms of relating—from weekend dates to fully-established trial marriage situations. They are experimenting with degrees of candor and openness in regard to what they are doing, thinking, and experiencing. They are concerned with experimenting with touch as a method of communication, with drugs as a way of expanding awareness, and of arriving at new perspectives.

All this means decision-making in quite a different context than that with which we customarily deal. As a counselor and as a person concerned with working with young people, I feel the best help I can give is to continue to emphasize the need both for the individual and society for the standard of building relationships in which there is love, integrity, responsibility, and maturity.

Fourth, *an openness to experiences and their meanings, which can then be evaluated and reviewed on the part of the counselor, is highly important.* The closed, secretive, disapproving character of the society as it presently exists needs to be ameliorated if the envisioned kind of approach to moral decision-making is to be made. This needs to be accompanied by a capacity to listen non-judgmentally and a willingness to learn. I would like to emphasize especially the importance of the counselor being a learner and a growing being in the counseling relationship also. In these times of rapid change and experimentation, what other stance is possible? The experiences of our students and the results they attain are certainly significant raw materials of learning and growth for those of us who are concerned with exploring accommodations which will fit the twentieth century.

Fifth, *the counselor will assume much more importance as an educator.* His major teaching method will need to be thorough interchange and dialogue rather than didactic declarations and dogmatic assertions. Perhaps here we should emphasize the value of the Socratic method of teaching.

Sixth, *the counselor will be concerned with values and hence will appraise the worth of possible courses of action.* He will recognize, however, that these value-choices are totally involving and exceedingly complex. This will keep him properly humble and prevent him from hurrying to preconceived and inflexible positions. He will recognize that usually there are several responsible alternatives which can be chosen within the guidelines of integrity and respect for the rights of others. The problems of racial accommodation, civil rights, and sexual patterns as they are developing in this country are good illustrations of today's moral issues which have great complexities about them, and which permit variations in the behavioral patterns associated with them.

Finally, *the emerging morality, if it takes the form I envision, will result in our viewing the moral-ethical aspects of our society in a very different way from what we do now.* The counselor's perspective will be greatly altered.

The emerging morality must deal with matters which influence our capacity to relate both in our primary relationship and on a world scale. Let me illustrate. One of our pernicious sins is that of labeling, a practice used in a most punitive way. We give someone a label with a negative connotation and we are then freed to do anything we choose to the individual. Someone, for example, is labeled a convict, a homosexual, a communist, or an atheist. Once this is done there is no escaping the label. Labeling is essential to the conduct of modern warfare. It is used by all the combatants, since it enables them to kill without compunction. We label our "enemies" as "communists"; they in turn label us "imperialist." If the same men were thought of as husbands, fathers, or sons, killing them would become an exceedingly difficult matter. But when we can deflect compassionate feelings by labeling, when we can turn a person into an agitator, a promiscuous individual, a sexual deviate, a foreigner, it becomes easier to kill him, to imprison him, to subject him to any kind of degradation we choose. How can labeling be anything other than an immorality?

Another immorality is that of clinging to the *status quo*, of using all possible tactics to keep things as they are. It is out of this rigidity and inflexibility that all kind of evils grow, or, being there already, grow faster until they are past the point of correction.

Unquestionably one of the elements which has made our present racial situation more acute, and which has contributed to its almost unsolvable characteristics, has been that for decade after decade we let an evil go uncorrected or even let it worsen. This blind and perverse clinging to the past constitutes a serious immorality. We find this kind of obstinancy in many places, in so many in fact that one begins to fear that this unyielding resistance to change will be our undoing. Our unwillingness to deal reasonably and rationally with our problems results ultimately in the necessity of coping with hatred and violence which have grown up about them and which make their solution well-nigh impossible.

An aspect of this same immorality is that of clinging to a mode of authority so archaic that all growth and change is stifled. I refer to the insistence upon holding to the idea of a transcendent, unchanging authority which provides an answer to all questions or issues. The inability to move away from this reliance upon a transcendent authority has contributed much to the weakening of organized religion. The issue of authority which now divides the Catholic church is reflected in the turmoil over the question of birth control. The report of the Pope's Commission which has been studying the position the church should take on this issue shows in a most interesting way the struggle going on within the church over the issue of authority. It contains both a majority and a minority report. The majority report makes a valiant effort to re-evaluate and redirect church thinking in the light of today's problems. It recognizes that:

> ... the social change in marriage, in the family, in the position of women, the diminution of infant mortality, advances in physiology, psychology, and sexology, a changed estimation of the place of sexuality in conjugal relations have helped bring a better, more profound and more correct perspective of married life and intercourse.

The minority report, on the other hand, has this to say:

> The church cannot change her answer [on birth control] because this answer is true. It is true because the church, instituted by Christ to show men a secure way to eternal life, could not have so wrongly erred in all these centuries of its history. If the church should now admit that the teaching is no longer of value, it must be greatly feared that its authority on almost all moral and dogmatic matters will be seriously harmed.

One of the Catholic physicians who advised the commission commented that "the debates have convinced me more of the intrinsic danger of an irreformable statement than of the intrinsic evils of contraception."

The whole issue of transcendent authority is intensely and sharply highlighted in traditional religious concepts, but it extends to other fields as well. I have already noted that workers in other fields are caught in the same trap—the tendency to bolster their own position with transcendent authorities. Having assumed that they have a final unchallengable answer, they find themselves unable to respond to new developments, findings or ideas. They have in a very real sense painted themselves into a corner.

Charles Schultz, in the cartoon strip *Peanuts,* caught the essence of the matter. Peppermint Patty was asking Roy for help. "What do I do," she asked "when I tell something that turns out to be wrong? I told what I thought was true but it turned out not to be. What do I do?"

"Well, you could admit you were wrong," Roy replied.

"Well, besides that I mean," was Peppermint Patty's response.

Another immorality is the perpetuation of hypocrises and deceits which become so monstrous that all capacity for trust and confidence is eroded, and all consistency is destroyed. Twice now we have had exposures of cheating scandals which have occurred at the Air Force Academy. The last time cheating was in the news I came across an editorial in one of our major newspapers in which the writer acclaimed the honor system as an exemplification of the American way of life. "If we can't make the honor system work in the Air Force Academy, what can we make work? We must make it function!" This certainly became a hypocritical expression when I remembered that in 1965 I had read in the Intelligence Report section of *Parade* magazine a release which stated that, "since 1958 the Red Chinese have shot down 10 reconnaissance planes belonging to the U.S. or Nationalist China." We are now sending over pilotless planes flying on pre-set, high-altitude courses which can be altered by radio command. "Naturally," says the Intelligence Report, "we disown the observation planes when they land on Chinese soil or are shot down over Red China. But they constitute our most valuable intelligence source in the Far East."

If the Air Force was to be consistent and support the procedures outlined in the *Parade* report, a rank injustice was then done the cadets at the Air Force Academy when they were punished or expelled for cheating. They should have been graduated with honors. Of course some of them were still not hardened enough in their patterns. "Naturally" they should have "disowned" any connection with cheating. But their behavior had promise and with practice should improve. They were showing a marked competency for the chicanery they are likely to be engaged in as Air Force officers.

This is, I think, the kind of immorality that has got our nation and our civilization into such serious trouble.

I would hope we all might have an experience similar to that of a Baptist minister I met in Italy in 1945 at the end of World War II. One day in reminiscing about his past professional activities he described the early years of his ministry. During this period he was apparently quite preoccupied with preaching against the evils of card-playing, dancing, and excessive use of cosmetics. Then World War II came along and he became chaplain for a division of men in the Army. He moved along with this group throughout the war, going through North Africa into Sicily and through the length of the Italian boot. This experience made a different man of him. Looking at it and contrasting it with his early ministry he remarked, "My, my, it has just altered my whole category of sins."

And this is what I wish for us. We, too, need to alter our whole category of sins. I am thinking not of rearrangement of various prohibited or acceptable acts, nor of developing a new code of behavior. I am concerned with creating those conditions and processes which enable us to come together in respecting, understanding, appreciative ways. I am concerned with integrity, with building trust and the capacity for openness and self-realization in relationships. I am concerned that the desire and ability for outreach be extended. I oppose those conditions and processes which erode trust, destroy communicative capacities, leave one isolated, and reduce confidence in the possibilities of working together. I disapprove and reject those experiences which now or in the long run place us in a prison of distrust, wall us off from others and make us distrustful of our own capacities and impulses.

Once again let us remember that the demands of the emerging morality are all-involving. We are all responsible for helping develop a truly moral situation, for thinking through what is involved in a genuinely humane ethic. I know that to accomplish what I have suggested, formidable obstacles will have to be overcome. This will not be easy. But I believe, in closing, I can do no better than to quote for you a statement I enjoyed when I came across it.

> It is a simple thing to say what we believe. And what a difficult thing, sometimes almost an impossible thing, it is to do and to be. But we can

bind ourselves ever more firmly to the vision of a truly ethical life. We can pledge ourselves, each in his own way, to strive to climb ever higher toward that level of life. It will not be easy. There will be discouragements and endless frustrations. And it will take courage, simple courage. Yet, as the epitaph in the ancient Greek anthology has it: A ship-wrecked sailor, buried on this coast, bids thee set sail; Full many a gallant bark, when we were lost, weathered the gale.

REFERENCES

1. Halleck, Seymour L. "Sex and Mental Health on the Campus." *Journal of the American Medical Association*, 200(8):684-690 (May 22, 1967).
2. "Conversations with Pope Paul VI." *McCalls*, XCV:93, 137-138, 141-142 (October, 1967).
3. Robinson, John A. T., *Honest to God*. Philadelphia: The Westminister Press, 1963.
4. Fletcher, Joseph, *Situation Ethics*. Philadelphia: The Westminister Press, 1966.
5. Kirkendall, Lester A. See *Premarital Intercourse and Interpersonal Relationships*. (Angora paperback) New York: Matrix House, 1961.
6. Girvetz, Harry, et. al., *Science, Folklore, and Philosophy*. New York: Harper & Row, 1966.
7. Maslow, A. H., *New Knowledge in Human Value*. New York: Harper & Row, 1959.

DISCUSSION

Panel

Panel Chairman: Dean ALICE LOW, *Grinnell College*
Dr. WILLIAM LYDECKER, *Gustavus Adolphus College*
HERBERT POSIN, M.D., *Brandeis University*
Dr. RICHARD KELLY, *DePauw University*
Dean CAROLYN JONES, *Albion College*

Dean Alice Low: To those of you who have not had an opportunity to read his prepared paper, you should realize that Dr. Kirkendall has only touched the highlights of his major thesis on the "Emerging Morality" in the limited time that he has had this morning. He has done the very thing that he said he did not wish to do—and that is to place the major emphasis on sexual relationships. I would like to suggest that those of us on the panel confine our remarks to questions or specific comments that will allow us in the time permitted to take advantage of Dr. Kirkendall's experience and give him an opportunity to develop his topic to a greater extent.

Dr. Kirkendall's remarks have raised in my mind some very important questions that are particularly pertinent from my own orientation as a Dean:

1. What are we, as deans and administrators, doing on our campuses to plan, lead, and project this on-going educative process of the student that is implied in Dr. Kirkendall's remarks? Nationwide, we are aware of the increasing demands for student freedoms. Are these demands being granted within an organized planned program with certain goals in mind or are we retreating step-by-step under student pressure?

2. If we really believe that during his four years on a college campus a student should go through the process of experimenting, testing, probing, challenging, demanding, criticizing, how do we set up that arena so it becomes a healthy, constructive part of his education?

3. Are we *really* listening to students to learn what their thinking is and what their needs are as they see them? Or are we still too rigid and inflexible in our own thinking to be able to interact in a meaningful way? Just as we must learn from the student, so must he learn from us. How are we doing this?

4. Dr. Kirkendall suggested the possibility that, in the not too distant future, we will no longer be discussing morality in the traditional sense but we will be discussing how we can move positively toward the realization of that which is best in our human potential. You probably are familiar with the novel, *The Harrad Experiment*, which has received a great deal of attention on many campuses. In addition to the sexual experimentation which is described in great detail, students are excited about the need for a "Course in Human Values." I only mention this because of the recognition by students that there is a great need for more than just casual and accidental opportunities to learn how to relate to people. Dr. Kirkendall suggested that if primary relationships were developed in a meaningful way, so does it become more possible to create understanding among peoples and nations of the world. It seems to me that people in personnel work and in counseling should be more concerned than anyone else with this aspect of a student's development. What are we doing in a structured way? Or what are we doing in an unstructured program?

It seems to me that if we do not address ourselves to the implications of Dr. Kirkendall's remarks, we will find ourselves in the same position as many college deans today—just coping with and not really contributing to the educative process.

Dr. Lydecker: I responded primarily to two aspects of Dr. Kirkendall's presentation: first, the implication that morality involves more than sex, and second, the point that a morality that focuses primarily on prescribed and proscribed behavior is inadequate in many ways.

I would like to address myself to the first of these considerations—that morality involves more than sex behavior. We must consider all kinds of relationship variables, for otherwise it makes labeling more likely and leads to the compartmentalizing of behavior. On this basis we are likely to have an individual who on the basis of a specific behavior considers himself perhaps to be a moral, upright individual yet in other ways behaves in ways that are immoral—certainly less moral than he sees himself in the sexual area. This might lead to a consideration of behavior in sales, advertising, and friendships in general.

I was also particularly attracted to the idea that man is essentially a social being who needs open and meaningful relations with others in order to develop his potentials.

Dr. Posin: It seems to me that certain aspects of the problem of morality have not been considered in Dr. Kirkendall's discussion. He has left out the problem of how the individual develops his moral sense, the content of that moral sense, and the quality of that moral sense. The first motivation for proper behavior in the child lies in fear of withdrawal of love. He learns further about proper behavior and thoughts from the ongoing example of his parents and other representatives of society. Examples by parents of honesty or morality, or the absence thereof, are very significant. He learns further from society's institutions such as schools and churches. He learns a lot of *do's* and *don'ts* in an automatic conditioned way without any thought or reflection. This determines the content of what later develops into his moral code. Its foundations are developed at a time when he is hardly able to think independently, using judgment, consideration, or reflection. By the time an individual is old enough to examine the moral code with which he lives, he is already encased in a structure with deep roots of many sources and with more or less rigid walls. There are, therefore, strong unconcious determinants to the development of our moral code and the style of our morality. I believe that what Dr. Kirkendall and others may think of as new morality is really the request that we examine this moral system of ours and subject it to critical scrutiny. Do I really believe this or that? Is it pertinent? Is it reasonable?

I think that the concept of encouraging love and consideration for others as a basis for the development of a moral system is an unimpeachable argument. To this, I think, one must add honesty with one's self. I think though that other elements from the person's past are important, not easily consciously accessible to the individual, but which also determine his moral judgments and how he goes about making them. If there is a new morality, it is not in the content of the moral strictures. That has always changed over the centuries. The newness lies in the way in which moral judgments are reached and accepted by the individual.

Dr. Kelly: I would like to emphasize that there are unconscious meanings and overtones behind the establishment of a set of standards that one might live by. As a result, it will be important to explore the internal meanings of a particular moral system along with the very important interpretation in terms of interpersonal relationships. I think that these internal dynamics will continue to play a significant role in counseling in the future. For example, let's consider the male whom Dr. Kirkendall describes as taking advantage of women. I think we need to consider this in terms of possible expression of hostility toward the female figure.

I believe there are many meanings to be found in interpersonal relationships that are not within the awareness of the individual.

Dean Jones: I would like to ask a couple of questions of Dr. Kirkendall. One of the challenges young people face today is the need to learn to live in a less structured society. Many things that were at one time considered as philosophical or moral absolutes are now being dealt with in terms of relatives. Rather than internalizing something because it is an accepted doctrine, present-day youth is asked in many cases to figure out what is best for him. The greatest portion of students I see in counseling are upset and confused because they have been exposed to such a variety of ideas and values on the liberal arts campus that they are no longer sure of what they believe.

What implications or problem does this emerging morality, in light of its relativeness, have for the student, the counselor, and the counseling service?

The other very practical problem I would like to deal with is that one of the advantages we have on a liberal arts campus is that just about everybody is involved in the counseling process. Assuming that we accept your approach to morality, obviously some changes will be necessary in the orientation of counselors in order to cope with this new definition.

How do you reach all of the people on the campus who are involved in counseling so that there is some similar approach to this to lessen the confusion and frustration that will result among the students when they face the traditional concept as opposed to the emerging morality concept?

Dr. Kirkendall: I would like to come to Dr. Posin's point first. He emphasized the negative motivations for behaving in a certain way which children may experience because of the potential withdrawal of love. I have a feeling that we have never really understood what is possible in the way of motivating behavior and developing standards by the extension of love.

I would like, also, to speak to Dr. Kelly's comment that morals are not always a rational process. Of course, this is so. On the other hand, we need to bring out these irrational processes so they can be examined and understood. This means that we are always in the process of learning. I don't think standards are set in the first five years of life and never, thereafter, changed. There is always the process of reasoning, developing, and reassessing, and this is what I think our schools and families need to encourage.

Dean Jones raised a point that I would like to comment on, too. She made a contrast between relatives and absolutes. I'd like to comment upon the possibility of universality. Rather than a pattern of behavior which is always absolute, I think there is a universality upon which we can depend. What is the character of the human being? I know we don't know too much about this, but I think that our social nature and needs are universal, i.e., the human being is a social being reaching out, wanting to ally himself, to find support—and give support. I think these are universals.

If the universal need is to realize our social potentialities, perhaps we can satisfy it in a number of ways as long as these ways provide the opportunity for us to get at basic social relationships which are necessary or needful. This is how I would get around that dichotomy you proposed.

Now, how are we going to lessen the confusion around this idea and the fact that so many are involved in counseling on the liberal arts campus? I don't really know. The more communication we have and the more basic we can get, the more we will come together in common insight, but I suspect that continuing confusion is going to be something we will have to deal with.

Dean Low: Do we have some questions from the floor?

Question: I don't think a liberal arts institution has any business wanting uniformity on the campus. And, indeed, most of the diversity is a kind of forum of dissent in which there is no absolute or final answer. I don't think there is much of a danger because the ones who have rigid, traditional, and authoritarian patterns to peddle will not reach many students.

Question: I would like to speak to that issue in a little different way. When we say that the problems are not ethical and moral ones but problems of relationships or psychological ones, this seems like psychological reductionism. I wonder how legitimate this is, because, at the heart of it, you are in fact offering it as an alternative ethical principle. Is a psychological definition of optimal interpersonal relationships an adequate criterion?

Dr. Kirkendall: What other criteria do we have besides the theological and the interpersonal or psychological one? What we need to do is to spell it out in broad terms to include the people who need this help. I hope that my concepts of human beings are broad enough so that I can see basic elements in the Christian religion and in a number of the other religions.

Question: I would like to ask if you don't think there might be two influences that are acting as guidelines for students as to how to use the sex act. One would be the new morality where there is a deep consideration and concern for the other, developing both of our human capacities, etc. And another influence is the more hedonistic playboy philosophy which says, "Yes, go ahead and use the sex act as a plaything for immediate pleasure." Would you not think that the playboy philosophy is winning out by virtue of the mass media: magazines and the cinema? Are there not these two influences going?

Dr. Kirkendall: Well, perhaps even more than two. But nevertheless I can see this dichotomy that you speak about. But, isn't this possibly what we are experiencing all the time with reference to many different aspects of relating? For example, I think, if my point of view is a valid one, that it means there is a need for coming together in circumstances where young people can be genuinely open and understood and where they can be authentic human beings.

Yet, our colleges and universities are growing in size and we are putting in more and more automation. We are growing more depersonalizing so that there are these counterforces. I would anticipate that there is no pure movement and that we will always have to battle counterforces.

SIDNEY M. JOURARD
University of Florida

Counseling for Healthy Personality*

● Man embodies possibilities for experiencing, achieving, creating, growing, and sheer enduring that the usual upbringing conceal from him. Modal upbringing shapes a man—it imposes limits on his experience and behavior—and it thereby produces men who are shadows of what they might become. If a man does not have some glimmering awareness that he can become more fully evolved than he now is, he is not educated. If a teacher or counselor does not believe utterly in the potentiality sleeping in all of us, beneath the crust of habit, that teacher or counselor is in bad faith, or else is ignorant of the sciences of man.

I have come to see counseling and psychotherapy, not as technical praxes, analogous to medical "treatment" or as a form of behavioral "training." Rather, I see these arts as more akin to an invitation to awakening, liberation, and self-discovery.

A counselor can choose to be a functionary for the social system within which he works, using his expertise to further train his "clients" (patients) for adjustment to the status quo; or he can choose to be more like a guide to, and exemplar of, healthy personality, inviting his clients to find *their* way to become more fully themselves. This paper can be regarded as an invitation to counselors to explore their own possibilities for transcending their training, to become more effective at inviting their clients toward fuller functioning as healthier personalities.

*Earlier versions of this paper were presented at the Cleveland Institute for Gestalt Therapy, in May, 1967; and at the meetings of the American Association for Humanistic Psychology in Washington on September 1, 1967.

II

People seek the help of a counselor when their lives have reached an impasse that nobody has helped them transcend. The symptoms of the impasse are incredibly diverse, including physical suffering, inability to concentrate, inability to overcome a persistent state of anxiety, depression, boredom, or guilt, inability to love another or to make love, loneliness, obsessions, anti-social behavior—the entire gamut of "psychopathology" as it is described in the textbooks of psychiatry and abnormal psychology.

Diverse though the symptoms of misery might be, they share one over-riding feature. They are the inexorable outcome of a way of life, a way of existing in the world, which informed common sense would tell us *must* lead to breakdown, to a "checking out" or a refusal to carry on with the way of life lived up to that point. We now know that the elaborate schemes for classifying "symptoms" of "mental illness" into neat categories is an unprofitable activity for would-be helpers of others. When we label someone "a schizophrenic" or a "neurotic" we lull ourselves into thinking we understand him before we actually do. The impasses in existence are only superficially described as illness, a term which at best is a metaphor, not an explanation. We spent centuries regarding people who "don't fit," whose behavior we could neither understand or accept, as "evil," or as "possessed by demons." It was indeed an advance toward greater compassion among men when the illness metaphor was applied to the people who wouldn't play the game of social existence as it was "supposed" to be played. But not all who, though physically intact, cannot or refuse to play the game are sick. Perhaps none are. As Szasz has graphically stated, "mental illness" is a myth, one that had a purpose but which no longer helps man regard and treat deviants and misfits as his brothers.

The persistent belief that people who "check out" or who "don't fit" are "mentally ill" and need to be "cured" of their disease symptoms beclouds understanding. To view one's "patient" or "client" or "counselee" as an exemplar of some category of disapproved humanity—schizophrenic, delinquent, neurotic, etc.—leads the would-be helper to treat him as *less than a full, human being*, less than a fellow traveller through this life. Anyone who has been treated by another, not as the very one he is, but as the embodiment of some category—a Negro, a Jew, a professor, a psychotic—knows that *he* is not being addressed by the person who so regards him. If I am regarded as "a patient" by "the doctor," and neither he nor I ever become acquainted with one another, we are doubtless both cheated, and it is questionable whether any enduring help can come out of so impersonal a transaction.

It is a more apt metaphor to regard the one in need of help as a *fellow seeker*. He seeks relief from his suffering, to be sure, and more fundamentally (whether or not he can verbalize the ultimate goal of his quest) he is seeking a way of being in the world, a way of being with others, and a way of being for himself, that is meaningful and rewarding; a way that produces satisfactions, hope, and meaning in further life rather than pain, misery, stultification, and impotence. These latter outcomes are *cries for help*. They are, as well, the proof that the seeker's way of life up to the point of breakdown, or refusal to carry on, was not compatible with wellness. It seems futile for a psychotherapist or counselor to "treat a symptom" in some technical way and then send him back to the very way of life that was inimical to truly human being. What is called for is not treatment but guidance, to help the seeker find some way to be himself that is more authentic, that yields growth and meaning in his existence. The counselor must aim to seek *with* his client and persist in the search until they jointly *discover* what changes in the client's self and world will permit him to live a life compatible with wellness. The helper, if he is to be more than a first-aid technician, must grope with his client to find healthy personality for him, that is, *a healthy way of being a person in the world* (the true meaning of "personality").

III

Healthy personality describes a way for a person to function in his world, a way which yields growth without placing other important values in jeopardy. A healthy personality shows evidence, in his very being and presence, of his alert and responsive care for himself. He finds his life meaningful, with satisfactions and some accepted suffering; he loves and is loved; he can fulfill reasonable social demands upon him. And he is in no doubt as to who he is, what his feelings and convictions are. He does not apologize for being the very person he is. He can look out on the world and see it from the standpoint of how it presently *is* (according to social consensus), but he can also see himself, the world, and the people in it from the standpoint of *possibility*. He can regard the world as a place in which he can bring into being some possibilities that exist only in his imagination. The world, the other person, and himself—none of these are seen by a healthy personality as sclerosed, frozen, finished, defined once and for all.

IV

Such a person has free and ready access to a dimension of human being much neglected by the "square," the hyper-conformist, the modal personality. I am referring here to something that has variously been called "the unconscious," "transcendental experiences," 'mystic experience." Actually, it is the experience of one's own, hitherto concealed *possibility*. This hidden dimension of the self, sought for centuries by men who have longed for personal fulfillment beyond conformism, is usually dreaded by the average person. When his "unconscious" threatens to speak, when direct experience of self or world invades his consciousness, he becomes overwhelmed with anxiety and may temporarily feel he is losing his mind and sanity. Indeed, he is on the point of "going out of his ego." His present self-concept, and concepts of things and people, are shattered by implosions and explosions of raw experience from within and without. He experiences his being in dimensions presently unfamiliar to him and hence frightening. But a healthier personality recognizes that his unconscious, this persistent but usually drowned out "dream," this source of new truth, is the voice of his true, real self, a statement of how he has mistreated himself (if the message is dysphoric), or an invitation to new possibilities of being for which he has become sufficiently grown and secretly, unconsciously prepared.

Wise men have always known that when the unconscious speaks, when fresh, transconceptual experience reaches awareness, it is better to pay attention. The breakdowns or check-outs that we have referred to are the final outcome of not listening. The symptoms and suffering are but the voice of the real self, the voice of a human being protesting so loudly it can no longer be neglected. Before the breakdown, the voice murmured softly from time to time, but the mur-

murings were in a code, a forgotten language that could not be understood. And so the person persisted in the ways of behaving, the ways of construing himself and other people, that had become increasingly good neither for his own growth nor his well-being. The healthier personality listens to his boredom, his anxiety, his dreams and fantasies, and gropes for changes in ways of meeting the world that will permit greater realization of potential self.

Healthy personality is manifested by a mode of being that we can call *authenticity*, or more simply, honesty. Less healthy personalities, people who function less than fully, who suffer recurrent breakdowns or chronic impasses, may usually be found to be *liars*. They say things they do not mean. Their disclosures have been chosen more for cosmetic value than for truth. The consequence of a lifetime of lying about oneself to others, of saying and doing things for their sound and appearance, is that ultimately the person loses contact with his real self.

The authentic being manifested by healthier personalities takes the form of unself-conscious disclosure of self in words, decisions, and actions. It is a risky way of being, especially in a social setting that punishes all forms of action and disclosure that depart from some current stereotype of the ideal or acceptable man. The healthier person will doubtless experience many a bruise, for being and disclosing who he is, but he prefers to accept these blows rather than lose himself, or sell himself (his authentic being) for short-run acceptability.

Indeed, there is much reason to suspect that authenticity before others is the same mode of being that permits a man to have access to the underground realm of experiencing, the unconscious. Defensiveness and concealment of self before others unfortunately are the same modes of being which screen off a man's unconscious, his preverbal experiencing of new possibility from himself. The currents of feeling, fantasy, memory, and wish that would get a man criticisms from others also produce anxiety in himself, and so he blocks these from the view of self and others in the service of self-defense. In time, he succeeds in fooling himself as much as others into believing he *is* the man he is so expertly *seeming* to be. In truth he is an "invisible man." Whatever is authentic of him, whatever is most spontaneous and alive is buried so deep not even he can cognize it. One of the reasons less healthy personalities are so self-conscious, so deliberate in their choice of word and action before others is that they dread "letting slip out" something which truly expresses their being, something which will get them into trouble. They are, as it were, idolators of the state of artificial grace known as "staying out of trouble." In fact, they have sold their soul and their growing possibilities for a good but false name.

All this is not to say that healthier personalities are always fully visible, fully transparent before the gaze of self and others. Such chronic self-revelation may be itself idolatrous, and is even suicidal in certain circumstances. Certainly we would expect a healthier personality to have enough common sense, judgment, even cunning, to preserve himself in a hostile environment, dropping his guard only when he is among trusted and loving friends. And, in fact, a healthy personality will have been able to enter into and maintain relationships of trust and love with one or more people, people whom he knows and responds to.

VI

Another dimension of healthy personality concerns the realm of values itself. Healthier personalities seek and find meaningful values and challenges in life, so there is an element of direction, of focus to their existence. Less healthy personalities, estranged as they are from their real selves, usually pursue only clichéd goals and values—money, security, status—presently current in their social milieu. These latter goals frequently do not challenge or inspire the average person to the fullest integration and expression of his unique being, they do not "turn him on" or keep him going and growing. The upshot is he will often feel trapped, or worse, feel that he is "losing his mind." The latter fear is most likely to occur when a person looks at the externals of his present situation, finds he has accomplished or has been given "everything to make a man happy," but, in honesty, is miserable, bored, and doesn't know what to do next. He has "loved ones," a family, material success, nice house, car, and so on, but finds his work increasingly boring, more like a treadmill; his relationships with others empty, formal, and all too predictable; and he entertains fantasies of murdering his loved ones, chucking it all, and going to the South Seas, only to repress these ideas with the anxious thought, "I must be insane to harbor such notions." He might scurry into further busywork, commence drinking to excess, create excitement by treading along primrose paths at great risk, or do other searching in the outer world for some new meanings. He looks in the wrong place, the right place being within his own experience. The healthier personality, less estranged and less afraid of his real self, can look within and without, and create or find new sources of value, new directions of commitment, even when these elicit some criticism from others in his world. He is freer to invest value in more aspects of the world than his less healthy counterpart.

VII

A healthy personality lives in and with his body, he is an "embodied self." He is not afraid or ashamed to touch his own body, or that of other people with whom he is on intimate terms. He is able freely to move his body, which has a look of grace, co-ordination, and relaxation. "He dances through life" (to state this idea in its most extreme but essentially accurate form). By contrast, the less healthy personality is afraid to live in his body. He represses his bodily experiencing, and feels his body alternately numb and dead, or as a dangerous and stinking cesspool charged with explosive nitroglycerine. He must take care lest an urge, a feeling, an impulse, a movement, break through the tight control. For him, this would be disastrous. One of the most common evidences of disembodiment is muscular tension that reveals itself as stiffness in body posture, awkwardness in gait, the mouth a thin red line, the jaws clenched, the face an immobile mask, frozen in false smile or anxious frown or counterfeit dignity; the voice emits sounds that are jerky, pressured, constricted. Touch such an average person on the arm, or place one's arm around his shoulder, and he will instantly stiffen, experience panic, jump as if stabbed, and perhaps experience a mixture of sexual arousal and guilt or anxiety. The healthier person has a more fully lived and experienced body—his face is mobile and expressive, he speaks in a voice that is free, not one which is fighting off an impulse to say something else at the same moment that the present speech is being emitted. It is no accident that average people receive psychotherapeutic benefit from instruction in vocalization, freely expressive dance, and from massage and other forms of direct experience with their bodies. Indeed, the therapists of the future will without doubt be obliged to learn to live gracefully with their own bodies, and to learn ways of inviting their clients to get back into theirs.

An important part of bodily experience is sex, the erotic impulse and feeling. Perhaps our puritanical avoidance of body-contact in everyday life is expressive of our mixed attitudes toward sexuality. A healthier personality is able to experience his erotic feelings without fear, and he is able to express them in a relationship with a chosen partner without needless inhibition, as part of the sexual dialogue. The less healthy person is usually so self-conscious he cannot "let sexuality happen" in his attempts at loving transaction, and so he tries to force matters. The result may be premature climax, impotence, frigidity, inability to know and to attune oneself to the sexual being of the partner, and so on. Likely, the beginning of a cure or liberation from sexual difficulties is made outside the bedroom, but inside the self.

VIII

We alluded above to the ability of healthier personalities to find and maintain relationships of love and friendship in the world. This ability insures that a healthier person will have access to relief from the existential loneliness in which we all live. Note that I used the term "relief." Loneliness is not a disease from which one can be cured; it is instead an inescapable fact of human existence. Less healthy personalities, cut off as they are from the fount of their real selves, find *themselves* terrible company. They cannot long tolerate solitude, and they run willy-nilly into busywork or superficial companionship with others. They do not, however, truly encounter another person and enter into dialogue with him. Hence, the feeling of loneliness, of not being known and understood, chronically nags at them as does a boil on the buttocks, or a stone in the shoe. The healthier personality, because he is less self-concealing and has readier access to his own fantasy, feelings, memories—his real self—is less afraid of solitude when that is his lot; and when he is with others, he can feel that secure in his own worth that he can let encounter and dialogue *happen*. During the process of such dialogue, the shell which encapsulates him as a separate, isolated being ruptures, and his inner world expands to include the received world of experience of the other. When the dialogue ends, he has experienced himself in the new dimensions evoked by the other person, and he has learned of the personal world of another—he is enlarged and changed. The less healthy personality defends himself against being so affected and changed in his contacts with others. He "rubs shells," or clinks his character armor against that of the other person, but does not meet the other. There is no encounter.

Just as a healthy personality dares to let himself be the one he is, so does he respect, even cherish and defend the "suchness," the idiosyncrasy, of the other person in his world. He eschews sneaky efforts to manipulate the feelings, thoughts, and actions of the other, and hence he truly experiences the other person as *an other*, as a source of being, different in some respects from him, and similar to him in other ways. The less healthy person dares neither to let himself be, nor does he trust the being of the other, when he is not controlling that being. In his transactions, he seeks always to influence the other, if in no other modality, then in the way in which he will be seen and experienced by the other. In the extreme instances of unhealthy personality, the individual actually (this can only be stated metaphorically) detaches his ego from his body and functions as a spectator and manipulator of his own depersonalized body as "it" transacts with the other person. This depersonalized body is then manipulated before the other, in the hope that the other's experience of and responses toward this counterfeit person can thus be controlled—robots performing before others who are perceived as robots.

IX

I have tried to convey some idea of what healthier personality looks like, at least in some of its dimensions. Now the question to be considered is, "How does a counselor go about guiding a suffering person in these paths?" First, let me set our discussion in a context.

As Marshall McLuhan put it, we have entered the "electronic age." There are encounters between people who never knew, earlier, how the other experienced this shared world and time. Confrontations between perspectives, which terrify or challenge the participants, are now going on.

This is also the age of growing automation. We are on the brink of untold leisure. Work is being done for us by machines supervised by other machines which are regulated by master machines. Increasing numbers of us have time on our hands. Our hands are idle. We keep them out of mischief with insensate busywork. Idle minds, liberated from obsession with thoughts about "getting it made," are likewise faced with challenge or threat because of automation. For millenia, man faced the challenge of securing his life and his livelihood and he did not ponder, "What is my life for?" If he mulled too long over this question, he might starve to death, or be exterminated by an enemy to whose approach he was inattentive. Now, and in the future, if he does *not* ponder this question and explore more of his locked-in possibilities (let his "unconscious" speak to him) he will not be able to endure his existence.

This is the social and historical context in which counselors and psychotherapists are asked to find a new place and social function as liberators and enlighteners, existential guides and explorers. In the brief eighty years that scientific psychology and psychotherapy have existed as self-conscious professions, the world has changed radically—through the collapse of the Victorian age, World Wars I, II, and the imminence of III; revolutions in every major nation and dozens of minor ones; man's invasion of space, and the discovery of "inner space." Every one of these events has had its impact on man's awareness of his own being, of other men's perspectives, and his awareness of the possibilities of the world. With every expansion of man's consciousness has come new problems of how to live, how to be, and how to pass the time.

Up to the present electronic and automated age, psychotherapists and counselors have truly been a specialized breed of socialization agents; their job has been to pick up where family, school, and other socialization agencies have failed, to complete the work of shaping up a citizen whose behavior would not be a problem to everyone else. People who didn't "fit" were called "Them," those who treated with them were called "We," or "Us."

We psychologists, clergymen, social workers, and counselors of all kinds were trained to view misfitting people, "Them," as sufferers from "mental disease," and we were led to believe that if we mastered certain theories and techniques for transacting with "Them," the patients, we would effect a cure. In this way, "We," the counselors and psychotherapists—solid, conforming, professional men with a stake in the status quo—served society, and we could take pride in the fact that we did it well, earning our money with hard, scientifically informed work. We always were pledged to foster and protect our patients' well-being, but curiously enough, our concepts of wellness were well-nigh identical with those versions of personality that would fit into the social system that subsidized us—with its established class structure and its resistance to change. Revolutionaries, anarchists, and rebels against the status quo (including hippies, poets, painters, and writers) could conveniently be seen as sufferers from unresolved Oedipus conflicts. We psychotherapists and counselors did not seriously view each man as a unique source of authentic experience, a perspective that in a more pluralistic, enlightened society might be *confirmed* rather than invalidated. We shared the short-sightedness of our established society, and called the officially sanctioned view of the world "reality-contact" and everything else madness or autism. From this view, people who wanted to make love, not war, are seen as impractical, schizoid, or seditious. No matter what our private sentiments may have been, we were unwittingly pledged to protect the status quo by invalidating the experience of those who found it unlivable. We called this invalidation "treatment." In effect, we were, and mainly continue to be, a peculiar breed of commissars: watchdogs over human experience, pledged to annihilate experiencing that is designated mad, and to seek to replace it by modes of experiencing called normal. Like it or not, there is a politics of psychotherapy just as there is, in Laing's* words, a politics of experience. It is instructive to realize that to many "hippies," counselors and psychotherapists are "shrinks" who "put you down by putting a tag on you." We are not seen as sources of help by many of this growing subculture.

X

Man can experience himself and the world in myriad ways. Being can be likened to a projective test. In itself, it is nothing. For man, as it discloses itself to his embodied consciousness, being can appear as well-nigh anything. The sun can be a distant star, or it can be the eye of a god evoking life wherever it looks. To insist it is one rather than the other is *politics*. To persuade a man that it is a star

*Laing, R. D., *The Politics of Experience, and the Bird of Paradise*. Penguin, 1967.

and not a god is to be a propagandist for some vested interest. We have been confirming what Freud, with incredible courage, found for himself—that our possibilities of experiencing are infinite, and infinitely beyond that splinter of awareness we acknowledge and call "normal" and disclose to others. In fact, to the extent that we find our own ordinary consciousnesses banal, we have an answer to a riddle: How was it possible for Freud, for so many years, to spend twelve to fourteen hours daily listening to people disclose their offbeat experiencing to him, without swooning from fatigue or boredom? One possible answer is provided by the experience of users of LSD and marijuana. Freud encouraged people to disclose their unselected experience, and I have little doubt that it "turned him on," it flipped him. His psychoanalytic practice was like a forty-year "psychedelic" trip, or forty years in a gallery of surrealistic art. Hour after hour, day after day, exposed to dreams, fantasies, memories that shattered his conventional rubrics and expectations about the human experience—it couldn't help but expand his awareness of his own being, and of the possibilities for experiencing the world. That highly prized state, "being normal," must have looked like banality and fraud incarnate to a man who had dauntlessly opened Pandora's Box and became privy to the secrets of expanded experiencing, which he found in himself and in those who consulted with him. Each disclosure from a patient must have exploded his concepts and expectations of what is possible.

I think that, in keeping Pandora's Box open, "We" have been infected, or perhaps it is better to say disaffected. "We" have been infected with the truth, that we *can* experience much more than we permit ourselves, and more than the guardians of the status quo would like us to. And "We" may have been disaffected from unthinking compliance to the established ways of living our lives, ways of relating to our fellows, ways of experiencing and living in our bodies. "We" are starting to study man-for-himself—for his possibilities of development and fulfillment that go beyond mere conformity with prevailing norms.

XI

In short, the truth is upon us. There is no more "Them"—only us, graspers and gropers after meaning in a social structure that aims to shrink our being, but in a world that requires us to grow. If we insist that patients and subjects belong in the category of "Them," then I, for one, have become one of "Them." I have come to believe that my task, as a psychotherapist, is no longer a specialized technical praxis, but rather that of an explorer of realms of experience and behavior, of ways to relate to others and to the social order that enliven me, that keeps me fit and vital, loving, responsive, and growing and inventive in the world, ways that evoke new possibilities for achievement, contributions, and enjoyment. My criterion of success in this quest is not solely whether my behavior appears "normal" to others; but, rather my *experience* of dialogue and encounter, of feeling free, responsible, potent, growing, and alive. The criterion of "success" has shifted from exclusive attention to behavior to the person's experience. I have been for too long aware that in appearing normal to others, I felt benumbed and dead within, a habit-ridden plaything of social pressures and expectation. And I have known too many people—fellow seekers (I used to call them patients)—who were exemplary in their conduct, but dead or desperate inside, and who could tolerate their "normal" existence only with the aid of booze or tranquilizers, or periodic hospitalization for ulcers.

A new specialist is called for in our time, and I believe those of us who presently are counselors and psychotherapists may be in the best position to grow beyond our training into the new role. I haven't an acceptable name for this specialist, but I see him as a westernized version of his eastern counterpart, the *guru* or teacher. We might call him an existential guide and explorer, a "psychedelic man," a consciousness-expanding expert, a growth counselor, a self-actualization agent, or a lover. He is a guide to more expanding, fulfilled, and more fulfilling ways to experience life as a person. He is a "world"*-shatterer and rebuilder. As such, he has a robust interest in his own fulfillment, and he pursues this, in part, by helping others to fulfill themselves. But part of his function is as an *exemplar* of a turned-on life, a revealer and sharer of how *he* has found his way. He is himself "reborn," in the Sufi sense, or awakened and liberated in the sense of the Zen masters or Taoist teachers. He is a Boddhisatva rather

---

*The term "world" is used here to refer to the way in which a person *experiences* the existence of the world: what he perceives and ignores, how he attaches meaning and value to the world as he experiences it.

than the Buddha himself—awakened, but not out of this world. Instead he remains in dialogue with those of his fellow seekers who are themselves seeking to become *men* rather than social functionaries. He shows and tells how he has been awakened, and serves as a guide to others. He is an experimental existentialist, literally. He experiments with *his* existence, seeking that way which generates maximum enlightenment, freedom, and love.

This view of a counselor or therapist as a *guru*, teacher, or psychedelic man has implicit in it an entire new theory of suffering, growth, practice, settings for practice, schools for training—the total paraphernalia of a profession. But first, it calls for an enlightened perspective on society, on one's role within society, and expanded views of human possibility that are authenticated by having discovered new possibilities within oneself. It calls for a "going away," and then for a return, renewed. It calls for a kind of death, and a kind of rebirth. You can easily see adumbrations with eastern philosophies, Jewish mysticism, early Christian existential (lived) theology, Marxist social criticism and utopianism, current existential phenomenology, and Freud's work in this perspective. Ancient myths about leaving home, to live and learn, then to come back, to establish dominion over one's kingdom are also relevant. From this standpoint, hippies and "drop-outs" have taken just the first step, the leaving. If they are men (and women), they will return, to renew and humanize the society they left.

XII

Let me see how far, in a brief overview, I can explicate some of this view of a new task for counselors and psychotherapists. I took part in a symposium at the Southeastern Psychological Association on "Innovations in Psychotherapy." My topic was to be "Going Away." The other panelists spoke, respectively, on Gestalt Therapy, Transactional Analysis, and Family Therapy. I intended to talk about retreats, meditation, and places of joy, tranquility, and enlightenment, like Esalen Institute at Big Sur. But I changed my topic after hearing the other panelists, and spoke instead about innovations in a psychotherapist—myself. I gave a brief account of what I have done with and beyond the very excellent training I received in order to become a psychotherapist, acknowledged as such by the public and by my colleagues. I spoke of the books I read, the impasses in my therapeutic work and personal growth, and how I transcended them; of the impact my experience as husband and father, colleague of others, teacher of students, research in self-disclosure and body-experience, my experience as one of "Them" (the patients) has had on my praxis as psychotherapist. I told how my realization that in our professional meetings, we therapists have limited our dialogue to ways in which we have succeeded in helping "Them" by trying out psychoanalytic techniques, Rogerian techniques, Ellis' techniques, Perls's techniques—but we have not deliberately acknowledged one another as *persons*, and shared our problems in staying alive and growing, and how we have addressed them; we have not deliberately explored or reflected upon the ways in which we behaved ourselves into sickness and out of it. Our "technologies" remain authorized ways to practice upon "Them" that, in principle, anyone can learn. As for myself, I have found, in my meetings with people who consult me, that "We" enter into dialogue, and my commitment is to help the other become more enlightened, more liberated from the bondage of habit, social pressure, the past, of some one mode of experiencing. To implement this project, I respond in any way and every way that is available to me in the context of dialogue. I guess I belong to no school, though I started in one. My commitment in the dialogue is not to a theory, technique, or setting, but to the *project* of abetting another person's wholeness and freedom and zestful meaning in life. Of necessity, there are technical ways of embodying this project, but these always reach an impasse, and at the impasse, the seriousness of my commitment receives its test: am I committed to my theory and techniques? Or to the project? In this context I don't hesitate to share with the seeker any of my experience with existential binds roughly comparable with those in which he finds himself (this is now called "modelling") nor do I hesitate to disclose my experience of him, myself, and our relationship as it unfolds from moment to moment. Nor do I hesitate, when it becomes relevant, to tell a joke, give a lecture for a few minutes on, say, my view of how he is being mystified by others in his life, and how he is mystifying others, thereby increasing his estrangement from his authentic experience. And I might give Freudian or other types of interpretations. And I might teach him such Yoga know-how or such tricks for expanding body-awareness as I have mastered, or engage in arm-wrestling, or hold hands, or hug him, if that is the response that emerges *in the dialogue*. I encourage him to try experiments with his own existence, like trying the risky business of authenticity, or changing living arrangements. Our relationship begins almost always in the seeker's expectation that it will unfold in a technically predictable and prescribed way (as outlined in popular books, TV, and movies). In fact, I feel pressure from him to keep me in an impersonal and technical role. I respect this and respond with the invitation to dialogue. If he accepts the invitation—and gradually he does—the relationship becomes a shared quest for ways he might live that generate wholeness, authenticity, freedom, vitality, responsibility, and self-respect and enlightenment. I do not hesitate to play a game of handball with a seeker, or visit him in his home—if this unfolds in the dialogue. In short, I've come to see that much of the rigidity of our professional practice is similar to an experimentally produced character disorder and character armor. The training which produces it serves to wean a person from those disorders, and that armor produced by his life with his family and his early schooling; but then it persists after graduate training as a *badge* as well as armor. You can usually tell where a person has been trained by his behavior with a patient. The technical ways of behaving we have called "psychotherapeutic practice" have relevance as authenticated paths to enlightenment and liberation if that is, indeed, what they have been for someone. But to congeal them as orthodoxies is to meet a seeker's hang-ups with hang-ups engendered in an academy. Technical approaches limit the capacity for response in dialogue, and confuse commitments. *A therapist is defined by his project*, not his means. The paradox I am discovering is that the most efficient means of fostering therapeutic aims is by sharing the fruits of *my* quest for fuller life (about which I am ultimately serious) with the seeker. This liberates me from technical rigidities. I experience myself as an explorer of ways I invent, or that others invent and I learn about and try, to make life fuller, freer, healthier, more meaningful for me, and who then share, show, and co-experience these ways with the seeker.

I don't think one can be trained to become this kind of psychotherapist-cum-*guru*-cum-teacher. It is rather a case of allowing oneself, first, to be brain-washed and trained into one ideology and praxis, then to allow growing experience to shatter or challenge it, in a dialectical moment of antithesis—and then to transcend the contradictions in a synthesis that becomes possible through a new commitment to more comprehensive goals. This is what Yoga and Zen are about—they are ways of shattering training, of bringing a person back to center, before commitments, so that he can draw upon more of his possibilities in new commitments. We have a Yoga of interpersonal relationships—dialogue is it. We have a Yoga of experiencing—meditation, art, and music may provide it. And we have a Yoga of goal-setting—spiritual leaders and exemplars provide this.

I think that in the future, the "compleat" counselor or therapist will have to tell the seeker whether he is a commissar, a trainer to the status quo, or a responsible liberator from congealed experience and the rigid, sickening behavior it mediates. Perhaps there will be joint practices, where Dr. John specializes in helping socially inept, "maladjusted," neurotic, and psychotic people (if we still use such dehumanizing jargon) manage acceptable social behavior. He will help the Incomplete Square to become boxed-in or bagged. Then Dr. Bill may take over, to liberate and awaken the seeker to more of his possibilities beyond those he has attained.

Perhaps, too, hospitals will be visited only by people who need a fracture mended, or a wound staunched. The community megahospitals can then be replaced by places where people can go *before* they sicken—when they notice the early signs that their life-style is sickening them—and where they can learn and be shown that experience and air outside our conventional rubrics can invigorate and renew. I think it is up to us counselors and psychotherapists to take those first exciting glimpses and those first bracing breaths.

REFERENCES

1. Jourard, S. M., and Secord, P. F., "Body-Cathexis and Personality." *Brit. J. Psychol.*, 46:130-138 (1955).
2. Jourard, S. M., "Self-Disclosure and Other-Cathexis." *J. abn. soc. Psychol.*, 59:428-431 (1959).
3. Jourard, S. M., "Healthy Personality and Self-Disclosure." *Ment. Hyg.*, 43:499-504 (1959).

4. Jourard, S. M., *Personal Adjustment. An Approach Through the Study of Healthy Personality*. New York: Macmillan, 1958. Second edition, 1963.
5. Jourard, S. M., *The Transparent Self: Self-Disclosure and Well-Being*. Princeton: Van Nostrand, 1964.
6. Jourard, S. M., *Disclosing Man to Himself*. Princeton: Van Nostrand (in press), 1968.
7. Jourard, S. M. (ed.), *To Be or Not To Be: Existential-Psychological Approaches To the Self*. Gainesville: University of Florida Press, 1967.

DISCUSSION

EDITOR'S NOTE: There was much interesting discussion of Dr. Jourard's paper, led by Dr. Milton Cudney of Western Michigan University. However, technical conditions caused by the podium light at the Holiday Inn speaker's table created sufficient interference so as to render the sound recording unintelligible. Hence we are unable to include this session in the proceedings.

PANEL PRESENTATION
EDUCATIONAL-VOCATIONAL GUIDANCE

LAWRENCE RIGGS
Wooster College

Extent of the Problem*

• The Educational Testing Service *College Student Questionnaire* last fall (1966) revealed that 16 per cent of freshmen men and 13 per cent of freshmen women in 307 American colleges and universities are undecided about their particular field of major study. The same percentages are undecided as to what vocation or occupation they would like to enter after completing their undergraduate careers.

In four-year colleges granting the A.B. degree, the percentages of freshmen undecided on majors included 19 per cent of the men and 13 per cent of the women. Those undecided about their vocational future amounted to 29 per cent of the men and 18 per cent of the women. Thus, more men than women are undecided in both of these categories. DePauw University reports for its freshmen classes from 1962-1967 percentages undecided about their majors ranging from 17 per cent to 24 per cent. Albion College reports its 1966 entering class had 26 per cent of the men and 18 per cent of the women who were undecided as to their majors, and 23 per cent of the men and 19 per cent of the women undecided as to occupation or vocational goals after college.

Judging from the college student questionnaire data reported in the College Student Profiles for 1966-67, 70 per cent of the men and 80 per cent of the women made their decisions on a major more than

---

*I would like to express appreciation to Dr. Joseph Heston for furnishing reports of his Bureau of Institutional Research and Counseling at Albion College from which much of the factual material in the early part of these comments is gleaned. Dr. William Wright of DePauw University furnished certain details concerning freshmen preferences for majors at DePauw University over a period of six years. I am indebted to him for this important assistance.

a year previous to entering college, with most reporting the decision was made more than one year prior to college attendance.

In making their initial choice of major, only 14 per cent of the men and 16 per cent of the women said that they had only one choice they had ever really been interested in. The balance had from two to four or more choices, with a great majority debating two or three choices. When asked who influenced them the most in their choice of major fields, the largest percentages (29 per cent for men and 38 per cent for women) indicated their high school teachers as being most influential. Other adult acquaintances followed, with 24 per cent of the men and 21 per cent of the women naming this source of influence. Men indicated their fathers to be of greater influence in this respect than their mothers, while women indicated their mothers to be more influential in *their* choice of a major field. In one of his reports, Dr. Heston comments, "This may come as news to parents who doubted if the children listened to either the mother or the father." It is interesting to note that people outside the home are named by the vast majority of both the freshmen men and the freshmen women.

The question arises: "How stable are these original choices of intended majors?" In a study of 1966 freshmen as compared to graduates of 1964-65-66, Dr. Heston found that at Albion College drastic changes are due in the area of science and social science majors. His data showed that the science aim may be about 30 per cent higher than the final actuality. In other words, he found that it would take 142 science freshmen to produce 100 science graduates with no allowance for any student attrition from college. The social sciences will take up most of the slack. For every fifty-nine entering freshmen expressing interest in the social sciences, it is possible to predict 100 social science graduates at Albion.

Data furnished from DePauw University indicates a similar drainage from the sciences to the social sciences, with the humanities majors about holding their own as in the case of the Albion report. There will be a few more humanities majors in both Albion and DePauw than are indicated by freshman choices.

In summary, these data indicate there are more undecided men than women, that many of the original choices were made three or more years prior to attending college, and that less than one-third of the decisions about majors were made in the year prior to attendance at college. Science majors are more frequently indicated than will be likely upon graduation, and fewer students indicate social science preferences than will ultimately have such majors. At both DePauw and Albion, and closely reflecting the national norms, approximately 80 per cent of the freshmen come with at least a tentative notion about their educational majors and occupational goals.

A number of comments should be made at this point about procedures in obtaining such information. At both DePauw and Albion attempts were made at one point to allow more freedom of choice, particularly allowing for a "no-choice option" to be expressed by freshmen. This resulted in a larger number of persons electing the no-choice option in each case. At Albion it was found that much of this reduction came in the social science area. In commenting on this phenomenon, Dr. Heston says, "Revision of a no-choice option after one or two years of academic exploration is certainly less traumatic than forced surrender of an unsuitable, prematurely chosen objective."

Further evidence of the instability of these early choices is shown in the analysis of the number of times that students change their majors prior to graduation. At Albion College nearly three-fifths of the seniors questioned made at least one change in the choice of their major department. It was felt that this evidence of goal change supports the wisdom of the new plan eliminating early indication of major.

In a discussion entitled "Flexibility in Approach to the Drop-Out Problem," Jefferson D. Ashby, Acting Director of the Division of Counseling and Assistant Professor in the Psychology Department of Pennsylvania State University (appearing in the *Journal of the Association of College Admissions Counselors*, Volume No. 1, pages 10-12), describes the activities at Pennsylvania State University in restructuring its educational programs "to increase the degree of flexibility that a student may have so as to reduce institutionally initiated pressures on the decision-making progress and to establish an extensive program of pre-registration counseling designed to assist students in formulating sound educational and vocational plans before they enroll in their first class." He reports that care was taken to allow sufficient flexibility in the programs so that, particularly in the freshman year, students without well defined plans will not be disadvantaged; at the same time students who have defined plans may follow courses of study in keeping with those commitments. He goes on to say:

> The University has also made it quite easy for students to effect changes in registration following participation in the pre-registration counseling program. After a student has had an opportunity to carefully appraise his interests, abilities, and achievements, and to gain a greater understanding of the varieties of programs which are available, where it seems appropriate a student may change his program of study by simply contacting the Office of Admissions and requesting such a change. Approximately 20 per cent of all entering freshmen make alterations in their initial commitment before they actually enroll in their classes.

Dr. Ashby feels that this and other provisions reported in his article are in support of the belief "that the University has clear-cut responsibilities to do all the things that it can to reduce the impact of institutional factors over which it has control in precipitating unnecessary drop-outs."

Part of my assignment in this program was to comment about the effect on freshmen of this lack of decision about the selection of a major. For lack of readily available sound data on this particular subject, I prefer to discuss the effects on students of requiring them to make an early statement of a major preference. It is my opinion that this is a potential source of much tension and anxiety both for the person who is forced to make a selection before he is really equipped to do so and for those persons who have a deep suspicion that they should know what their major field is and have a sense of inadequacy when they are unable to clearly state an academic, professional, or occupational goal.

It seems to be desirable for colleges to place emphasis on the importance of self-understanding, evaluation of one's interests, abilities, and aptitudes, and upon achieving education as a personal investment in growth, rather than placing emphasis on a vocational goal or a particular major during the freshman year. In my own counseling experience I have become aware of the large number of students who develop feelings of inadequacy and failure when they compare themselves to those disgustingly sure persons down the hall who somehow have easily and quickly settled this complex matter of academic and vocational choice.

I would like to make a number of observations which time will not permit me to elaborate at this point.

1. Insofar as we are talking about a liberal arts education, it would seem to me important that we place the emphasis upon understanding oneself in one's setting and making realistic appraisals of both the self and the setting. I hope that it is one of the important results of the liberal arts involvement that a student learns to know himself better and to modulate his relationships with his school environment, his community, and with society at large.

2. We should remember that many college graduates eventually do not work in the field of their undergraduate major subjects. Perhaps we should make this observation more frequently to freshmen. This is not to underestimate the importance of having some field of major concentration in the undergraduate years, but it is to emphasize the potential flexibility of the human creature as he grows through the life-long process of education.

3. Specialization comes soon enough. It is my personal opinion that every effort should be made to keep it at a minimum at the undergraduate years, especially in the first two years.

4. Change, flexibility, adaptability are words of the day in business and industry. Automation, new developments in methods, our sophisticated computerized techniques all point to the need for persons who can adapt to change and who are flexible as they apply their skills, understandings, and knowledge to the work of the world.

5. One study of liberal arts graduates (DePauw University) showed that they changed jobs two and one-half times in their first ten years out of college.

This leads me to make a number of proposals, many of which, of course, will be a summary of the material presented thus far.

1. We should initiate a positive campaign to eliminate from our questioning of high school students such a narrow reference as to make them believe we think they *ought* to know what career or what major field they *should* be studying; and secondly, we should eliminate any trace of the suggestion that there is only *one right job* existing in the world for them as individuals. The truth is (and we should begin to share this more widely) that every person can be happy and moderately successful in more than one occupation.

2. When these young people arrive on the college campus, I hope

we can school ourselves to ask (if we must inquire) whether they have *thought* of a major field of interest rather than asking them to name a field of interest, as though as we expect a specific response.

3. Somehow we must learn to emphasize to high school students and to college freshmen that personal discovery, involvement, personal development, and adaptation to a new and complex environment are significant goals for at least the freshman year in college, rather than vocational and academic decision in terms of major emphases.

There is something drastically wrong with our educational system if new insights do not develop as the student progresses through his college years. Students should not be made to feel uncomfortable about these changes. As a matter of fact, I hope we can gracefully let these young people know that we mature, seemingly secure adults have the frequent experience of introduction to new ideas, to new skills and techniques, and that this is a life-long thrilling and challenging process. An illustration of this happened to me this past week when I was reviewing an application for a Fulbright Scholarship and ran into the casual comment that the student wanted to study anthroposophy. I was most grateful that he went on to explain what it was; because I am fearful that my limited office dictionary might not have included this term which, I confess, was a new one to me. I am quite sure that, as a freshman, this young man had absolutely no idea that eventually the field of anthroposophy would be his choice for specialization in his senior year.

There is a challenge implicit here in imaginatively developing means for the furtherance of personal discovery and personal involvement in a new environment. I wonder if we can respond quickly enough and effectively enough to the needs our young people seem to be showing for this kind of flexibility. I suspect that they are ready for more flexibility than we are able to present.

4. In the next place, I think it is important for us to make available to students prior to the sophomore year objective means of self-evaluation in the form of testing and appropriate interpretation through counseling. I hasten to say that this is not to place exclusive emphasis on the value of tests, because I feel their ultimate value is only in using them along with many other things we know about individuals; but we do have an obligation to bring the best possible

techniques to bear in helping in this process of self-evaluation and discovery about the world of work. This should not be a wholesale approach. Not everyone needs or can benefit by testing.

5. I propose that we de-emphasize the idea that everyone should go to graduate school and that we begin to talk to freshmen in these terms, opening up valid alternatives, especially for women who neither want to teach nor go to graduate school for other programs.

6. We should make it easy to change an advisor and to change a major within reasonable limits.

7. All of this requires the development of specially prepared persons to counsel freshmen. In light of budget pressures, teaching load distresses, and an increasing feeling in some segments that faculty members ought not to be bothered with this kind of counseling, many of our colleges may be missing an opportunity by not giving careful preparation to some upper-class students to assist in working with freshmen in terms of their academic choices. I know this would cause some departmental chairmen to fear they might lose majors in their departments; but in light of all the shifts indicated in the data presented earlier, I think this is hardly a justified concern.

8. Much of the data we have reviewed strongly suggests we should foster opportunities for freshmen to meet and know what Dr. Heston refers to as those persons who are "important others" on the campus. Revealed through a number of studies of the influence of college atmospheres is the probability that role models are, indeed, still important even on the college campus. We should eliminate the notion that these confrontations ought to be only on the subject of a choice of major. It might well be that a choice of major is in some cases an important by-product of meaningful personal relationships.

9. Finally, I would go so far as to suggest that we not urge an indication of major by freshmen and that we not assign faculty counselors in relation to possible choices of majors for the first year at college. While important exceptions do exist in those cases where there is a happy coincidence of interest, aptitude, self knowledge, and opportunity, I feel we ought to view our freshmen as growing, dynamic, changing persons for whom an early channeling into one field would be a serious breach of academic integrity in light of what we ought to know about people and about the academic world. If we could ever achieve this, and along with it arrange all possible oppor-

tunities for the development of stability in personal relationships as a basis for meaningful changes in values, I believe we would make progress toward a more adequate basis for final judgments about major fields.

This is a complex subject. I suspect that many of our campuses do not have as complete information as is available at DePauw and especially at Albion. I furthermore suspect that even for those having the information, acting upon the implications may present serious problems.

ALBERT W. DAVISON, JR.
Denison University

How to Provide Occupational Information and Still Be a Counselor

● Leo Goldman, writing in *The Personnel and Guidance Journal* about the changes in quantity and quality of information, states:

> Counselors will be hard-pressed to keep up, not only with the sheer volume of new information, but with the forms in which it will appear—film cartridges, closed-circuit television, computers, and other media. One may well wonder whether it will be necessary to have full-time personnel who will do nothing but specialize in the acquisition and dissemination of guidance information....
>
> Because the new information is printed, is in tabular form, or appears on a screen or computer-operated typewriter, pupils and parents may attribute to it a greater degree of validity and reliability than is warranted (1).

So much has been said and written about the sources of occupational information that it would be difficult for me to add anything new to what you already know. Instead, I would like to direct my remarks in a slightly different vein.

The explosion (I would agree that this term is overworked) of occupational information has occurred, and each day's mail attests to the fact that the fallout has begun. Most of us in any given week receive reams of company newspapers, annual reports, recruiting brochures, sample books, calendars, statistical analyses, motion pictures, film clips, long-playing records, tapes, visitation offers, matches, ball point pens, pencils, gifts of the month, and on and on *ad nauseum*. Like many a business man, I hate to be away from the office because I know that when I return my desk will be piled high with "professional" mail. If the counselor is being snowed under by this avalanche, imagine the confusion it causes the counselee.

It is common for a college placement or career planning office to display occupational literature in racks, cabinets, or open filing cases. Some subscribe to commercial information sources that provide large amounts of codified material. In any event—and Goldman has a point here—someone has to evaluate and screen this material for it to be of workable value. Secondly, and perhaps more importantly, what is the real worth of any occupational information, no matter how attractively it is displayed, if it isn't used by students? How many of you, I wonder, have had seniors stop by your office and say, "I had no idea anything like this existed on our campus," or words to that effect. This situation may be more typical of colleges like Denison that do not require senior registration in the placement office. Consequently, only about 30 per cent of our men and about 50 per cent of our women ever visit the placement office. The majority, who are planning to go to graduate school, are advised (not necessarily counseled) by the Graduate School Counselor (divided responsibilities at Denison). Even in the case of those planning graduate work, I am informed that few take advantage of the information provided for them in the graduate school office. As is the case in the secondary school, apparently the college counselor cannot assume that the average student is self-directed enough to take advantage of the information readily accessible to those who make the effort to enter the portals of the Counseling Office. You, as counselors, must often be effective publicity agents. You must get the word to students that you do have helpful information available in your office and that this material can be obtained without too much effort. (I may sound cynical here.) How you do this must be tailored to your respective institution. You do, however, have a golden opportunity to introduce occupational information every time you counsel a student. If this material is used as an integral part of the counseling session, the counselee, in my experience, tends to regard it with interest and concentration. One caution, however: whatever you use, whether it be brochures, briefs, reports, or job descriptions, be sure you have at least scanned the material in advance. This effort on your part can prevent many an embarrassing situation.

I'm sorry to have to say that occupational material has been a means of buck passing as handled by some counselors. While it's obvious that the counselor cannot be an expert about every entry occupation or profession, he owes it to himself and to his counselees to be reasonably well acquainted with current trends in the fields attracting the majority of the graduates of his institution. In this regard, I have found the *Occupational Outlook Handbook* and its supplements to be extremely useful. What a mistake it is to load a student down with pamphlets about occupation "x" with no other interchange. This common procedure is an easy out for the counselor. The chances are that even if the student reads the material, he won't understand it or believe what he does understand. Leona Tyler reports that her research has found that "almost two-thirds of them [selected samples of occupational literature] ranked in the very difficult or scientific levels. . . . About the same proportions fell into the dull and mildly interesting categories" (2, p. 120). Apparently, the credibility gap extends into other areas outside the government.

Perhaps the most important issue associated with the mass dole of occupational information is the lack of the interpersonal relationship that should be a part of any counseling service. Often a student's request for information may be a convenient vehicle leading to the disclosure of a deeper problem which may or may not be of a vocational nature. I think most of you would agree that vocational counseling is closely related to the self image of the student as he perceives his role in society. I cannot see how the psychological need structure of a young person can be satisfied by means of a printed brochure.

Comments on GRAD

GRAD, or Graduate Resume Accumulation and Distribution, as most of you know, is the computerized placement system operated by the College Placement Council of Bethlehem, Pennsylvania. Designed to serve job-seeking college graduates, the system is just over one year old and will soon be "the world's largest repository for college-trained talent," according to the 1968 College Placement Annual. A new system, SCAN (Student Career Automated Network), is in the experimental stage. Similar in design to GRAD, SCAN will permit undergraduate students to place resumes in the pot for evaluation by potential employers. SCAN is a sort of early warning system that will enable college recruiters to locate talent before each year's formal recruiting season begins on the college campus. Both systems work essentially the same way. The candidate fills out a standard resume that, after validation by the college placement official, is sent to the CPC Data Center. There is no cost for this to either the applicant or the college. The resume is then placed in the computer system where it can be retrieved either by written request or by "on line" telecommunication. For this service each participating employer pays a fee, resulting in a code number that permits access to the computer memory. Those firms "on line" are provided with an enquiry program that supplies the user with a print-out of all candidates filling a given job description in a matter of minutes.

My observation has been that GRAD is more effective in the placement of technical personnel than it is for the liberal arts major. In fact, I strongly suspect that the system was conceived, born, and nurtured by the current and projected shortage of technical manpower. The competition by companies to hire engineers or scientists has reached fantastic proportions. The development of SCAN would seem to support this contention.

Coming from a liberal arts college where about 65 per cent of our seniors go on for graduate or professional degrees, I must confess that placement is becoming a minor problem. For example, last spring fifty companies interviewed fifty-seven of our senior men (out of a total class of 203 men). Of these, about thirty could be considered as being serious about immediate placement. The remainder preferred to mark time until called by Uncle Sam. If SCAN proves to be an effective placement too, then my function as a placement officer may dwindle drastically. I'm not particularly concerned, though, for like most college administrators I wear many hats.

Women's placement, outside of education, is more anxiety producing. In spite of what you may read, salary discrimination still exists and presents a morbid picture to the liberal arts woman when she goes job seeking. GRAD hasn't been of much help because, while not specifically excluding women, most enquiries almost spell out "Men Only."

Lack of feedback has been GRAD's principal deficiency. Last year, ten Denison alumni were referred to the service. At present, I have no record of those who were successful in finding a new connection. Each member institution receives a periodic print-out of the number of enquiries for each referral, but we are not notified when placement occurs. This situation is a major concern to most college placement officers and, undoubtedly, will be remedied.

As far as I'm concerned, GRAD, with its limitations, has given—and SCAN should give—graduating seniors much more exposure to potential employers than any single placement office can offer. What both systems do not provide the student is professional counseling and personal concern. To my way of thinking, the method of placement, whether it be by computer or recruiter, is of secondary importance. Most of us here today represent colleges where a one-to-one relationship with students is still possible. This is surely a precious possession. It seems to me that if we accomplish what we should as counselors in helping our young people to establish realistic goals and personal identity in a competitive society, then we should take advantage of every means at our disposal to accomplish this end. The computer, rather than being a threat to vocational counseling, should be viewed as a friendly ally, for the time freed by it allows the counselor to preserve and strengthen interpersonal relationships with students. Speaking for myself, I'd much rather spend the working day counseling than in any other way.

Summary

It may sound as though I'm trying to defend the role of the counselor in the information providing situation, and I must admit I am. In summary, what do I have to offer in the way of advice?

1. Screen the material you receive. If you can't do it yourself, assign the responsibility to someone in your office. Keep the material up-to-date. If it isn't used, throw it out.

2. Publicize the fact that the information is available in the counseling office by means of the college newspaper, bulletin boards, vocational seminars, etc.

3. Keep the faculty informed about the type of material you have available. Invite them to supply you with information pertinent to their fields of interest.

4. If compulsory registration is not a factor (or even if it is), encourage students to discuss their plans with you, using vocational

information as an integral part of the counseling interview, not as an end unto itself.

5. Use the material to stimulate the student to seek out alternative sources of information. Don't set yourself up as the only and/or "expert" resource.

6. Evaluate continually the validity of the information you have in your files. One effective means of doing this is to survey recent graduates, asking them to describe in detail what they are doing on the job. When compared with printed occupational briefs, the resultant correlation is often surprisingly low.

REFERENCES

1. Goldman, Leo, "Information and Counseling: A Dilemma." *The Personnel and Guidance Journal*, 46:43 (1967).
2. Tyler, Leona E., *The Work of the Counselor*. New York: Appleton-Century-Crofts, 1961.

JOHN R. THOMPSON
Oberlin College

Personality Correlates in Educational-Vocational Guidance

● The reader is immediately warned that the author is eminently qualified to speak on the topic of personality correlates of educational and vocational guidance. Among other things, these qualifications include the fact that the author does a minimum, if any, vocational-educational guidance counseling. The office of placement and graduate counseling, along with the office of the associate dean of the college and the associate dean of the conservatory, provide the bulk of vocational and educational guidance on the Oberlin campus. While students do seek vocational counseling in the psychological services, they are generally referred to members of the psychological services staff other than the author. In particular, one staff member is responsible for active consultation and liaison with the other offices on campus doing vocational and educational guidance. He then sees the bulk of students who come to the psychological services for vocational-educational guidance.

Secondly, the author is trained as a clinical psychologist. Although he has held the title of clinical and counseling psychologist, correlations between titles and training leave much to be desired. This lack of training and lack of experience further means that the author is not highly acquainted with the recent literature in the field of vocational-educational counseling.

The following remarks on the relationship between personality correlates and vocational-educational guidance are couched in the framework of four points. An attempt is made here simply to touch upon those areas where the work in the field of personality might well touch, overlap, and interrelate with work in the field of vocational-educational guidance.

No attempt to define what we mean by personality will be made. The reader can use what Donald Super (3) has called a "trait psychology approach" or a "social-role approach" or a "phenomological approach" to the definition of personality. It would seem that any of those definitions would be appropriate to the remarks that are to be made in this paper.

1. Vocation and Personality

It is possible to consider at some length the importance of vocation to personality. In our society it is rather evident that what the person does seems to be utterly important to our perception of him as a person. Individuals in our society gain status and at times have their self-concepts completely intertwined with their vocation or occupation. The perceptions others have of us seem to be intimately related to our vocation or occupation. For example, if we say we are a psychologist, then we might notice that people wince a bit and come out with statements like, "I hope there is nothing wrong with me," or "I hope that you won't analyze me." If we say we are the dean of students, we might notice that the other person seems somewhat confused; he wonders what a dean of students is or does. He thinks he has some idea of what a dean does but what is a dean of students? If we say we are the college president, then people don't know if they should call us Mr. President or His Excellency or what. If the plumber comes to our house and he is neatly groomed, a rather lean man, in starched shirt and trousers, rather rigid, compulsive in his manner and uses perfect English in a rather clipped fashion, we start thinking something is wrong. That's not our stereotype of the plumber's personality.

All of this is simply to say that here is one aspect in our interpersonal relationships where vocation seems to merge and be interlocked with our personality.

2. Personality and Vocational-Educational Choice

The fact that our personality seems to be so interrelated with our vocation or that our "self" is so tied in with our vocation raises the whole issue of the relationship between personality and vocational-educational choice. I'm not going to bore you by listing in length or reviewing the wide literature in this particular area. Instead allow me to summarize with this generalization: At this time we probably do not have any clear-cut relationships between personality traits and vocational preference which would be of practical significance in predicting vocational choice, success, or satisfaction.

Raylesburg (1) demonstrated that people can perceive a variety of roles in any one occupational category. For example, one student considering engineering can see the field as a scientific occupation. Another student thinking of engineering can see it as a materialistic occupation, and a third could consider engineering as a social welfare occupation. It would seem that man has the capacity to see in his job what his personality needs. There is the story of the young man who wanted to be a bum and his mother wanted him to be a doctor—so he grew up to be a bum doctor.

It would seem that we can perceive any one specific occupation as satisfying a variety of personality needs. Nevertheless, in working with students' vocational and educational choice problems, it would seem most worthwhile to attempt to ascertain how that student sees any particular occupation. Does he see it as scientific, materialistic, as a social welfare occupation? How does he see any particular vocation satisfying some of his own personality needs?

Certainly Small, Sweat, and Von Arnold (2) suggested with some of their data that if we define occupations narrowly and precisely by attending to functional specialities within occupations, we could find some significant personality differences in occupational groups. However, we are not at the point where we can specify any kind of high correlations between personality and vocational-educational choice. Thus, I think that our general statement that personality traits and vocational preference do not have any clear cut relationship that is of practical significance in predicting vocational choice, success, or satisfaction is still a fair statement.

3. The College Student and His Personality Correlates of Educational-Vocational Choice

Let me suggest at this point that we cannot separate the college student's educational-vocational choice from the other things that are going on in his life during his college years and during the time when he is thinking about and struggling with making an educational-vocational decision. What I am saying is that we cannot separate his educational-vocational choice from his "identity crisis" problems, from his "dependent-independent" conflicts, from his "becoming a person" in Roger's terms, "his self-actualization" in Maslow's terms, or from his normal development.

We assume that a person's occupation or choice of occupation or even his choice of an educational goal is of significant importance to his self-concept, his personality, and his identity. I don't think that this assumption is necessarily self-evident, but I'm willing to accept it at this time.

Now let's look at some examples in these particular areas. Let's start with the identity crisis. When the student is asking himself such questions as, "Who am I?" "What am I?" "What do I think is important?" I think we'll have to agree that his occupational choice (his educational choice) plays a relatively important role in answering some of those questions. If you go around asking people, "What are you?" I'm pretty sure that you will find they give you their occupation. Our vocation or occupation seems to be such an integral part of what we are that it is placed above being a husband, a father, and a human being. When people first meet and start becoming acquainted with one another, one of the first questions they seek an answer to is the question of what do you do, i.e. your occupation. If you are a woman they are interested in what your husband does for a living. Your standing in a particular group is dependent upon your vocation. The woman's standing in any group is dependent upon her husband's occupation. This kind of emphasis and the importance of vocation in our social relationships is certainly evident to the college student. He has been raised in this milieu and the identity he is struggling to find might well be highly related to his vocational-educational choice.

Now in some respects a change is developing in our society in which more emphasis is being placed upon humanistic interpersonal relationships and less upon vocation. One could interpret some of the present student movements as pointing the way to the development of social interactions which are not so highly dependent upon vocation and status-oriented vocations as has been true heretofore. The "hippie" movement might be an example of a situation where the individual's identity and status is not at all related to his vocational-educational role or to his ability to be a high consumer. This is not to say that the vocational-educational choice is still not related to personality, for I think that in the bulk of the students with whom we have to deal it is impossible to separate identity crisis problems from vocational-educational problems. It is unlikely that the student who seeks vocational-educational counseling is not at the same time struggling with some aspects of his identity crisis problems.

Secondly, it might not be uncommon to find that the student who is struggling with his vocational-educational goals is also at the same time struggling with some independent-dependent conflicts which are so common in the adolescent years. In many respects the college years are highly designed to bring to a head the dependent-independent conflicts, and the student at college starts on the road of modifying the emotional ties he has with his parents and developing a sense of independence. Individuals in the college age group will frequently express their strong desires for independence while at the same time they readily admit their fear of "going it alone." These dependent-independent conflicts are exemplified by the adolescent at one moment insisting he be allowed to do it himself and at the next moment being angry because we didn't do it for him. The independent-dependent conflicts are exemplified in the adolescent by his strong cry for wanting freedom and independence and at the same moment complaining that college rules are not clearly and specifically defined.

These dependent-independent conflicts in the student may well create at least two problems for vocational-educational guidance. First, the student might well want us to make his decisions for him. In this respect, he either openly or implicitly tells us that he wants us to tell him what he should do. In many respects he is asking us to assume responsibility for him and for his vocational-educational choice. By working through this kind of problem with a student we are not only helping him make his own vocational-educational choice but we are probably at the same time helping him resolve some of his problems with his dependent-independent conflicts. Should we go ahead and make the choice for him, we deny him the joy and opportunity for assuming responsibilities for his decision. If we make the choice for him, it is we he can blame if things don't turn out as he hoped. If he makes the choice himself then he must take the consequences of his decisions and has only himself to blame.

Now I think it is in the area of independent-dependent conflicts that we run into the problem of the student asking us to side with him against his mother and father. He wants some support to tell his parents that he wants to become something other than what they had hoped. We probably do not find this an uncommon problem. The student has started college with the idea of becoming what his parents have suggested and then he may decide he must change his vocational choice and wants to become something else. He may want us to help him "buck" the parents. I suggest we not be led down the wrong path. We deal here with the whole problem of the student starting to break away from the family ties, starting to enter a period of what might be called "emotional isolation" where he no longer turns to his family for emotional gratification. But he has not yet developed the skills or the relationships necessary for obtaining strong emotional support from peers and is perhaps heading into his identity crisis. That's one whole host of problems related to the dependent-independent conflict and related to personality correlates of vocational-educational guidance.

The second whole problem centers around what his parents want him to become. Here I submit it is not that his parents want him to become a doctor or an engineer or a lawyer. I think we sometimes make the error of thinking the parents have in mind a particular vocation or occupation. But more to the point might be that the parents have in mind certain personality-social aspects of the occupation. It is not the M.D. they want their son to become but the kind of individual they perceive the doctor as being. In this sense they are not telling their son or daughter to become a doctor but they are telling their son or daughter to become a certain kind of person with particular kinds of status, authority, position. And frequently it might well be that what they want their son to become is what they have never been able to be in their own personality. In this sense it might be well worth discussing with the student just why his parents want him to become something or other. It might be important to attempt to explicate just *what* the parents are asking of their son or daughter.

4. Counseling or Psychotherapy

Let me complicate matters even more. There are situations where the student comes to us for vocational-educational guidance as a first or a possible step toward seeking treatment for a highly disturbed condition. The student may be seriously concerned that he is badly psychologically upset but fearful or unwilling to consider that possibility. He thus just wants to brush shoulders with some kind of psychological help. Now the campus attitude toward vocational counseling and toward psychotherapy might make some difference as to whether or not the vocational-educational counselors get a preponderance of "hidden problems." If vocational-educational counseling on your campus is an accepted aspect of the student's life, but psychological disorders and seeing a psychologist or psychiatrist is not so readily accepted, then I would suggest that the professional guidance counselor has to be most alert to the problem of students coming for psychotherapy but doing it under the guise of vocational-educational counseling. Students are well aware that vocational guidance counselors have various kinds of psychological tests and the student may be slowly and carefully trying to find out just how disturbed he is.

There are times when the vocational-educational counselor has gone through the whole process of the initial interview, testing, interpretation, discussing, more interviews, and still the student seems unable to reach a decision. In some respects this behavior might be related to independent-dependent conflicts. On the other hand, it may well be that we have missed the boat. It may well be that the student is hanging on because he is trying to tell us something more. It may be that he is hanging on because he is trying to tell us that he wants us to find the pathology that he is trying to hide and to help him face it.

All of this is simply to say that in considering personality correlates of vocational-educational guidance, we have to face the fact that some students may come to us because of a severe neurosis or an impending psychosis. It may take us some time to catch on to that fact, but I think we have to be ready to handle that exigency.

Summary

In educational-vocational counseling it is impossible to avoid the problem of the student's personality. We have to hold in view the integration of the whole person. Frequently we will not have to laboriously attend to personality dynamics in our counseling, but other times we will have to take into account adolescent adjustment problems as well as be prepared to identify severe neurotic and psychotic conditions.

REFERENCES

1. Raylesburg, P. D., "Personal Values as a Frame of Reference in the Perception of Some Aspects of an Occupation." Doctoral dissertation, Teachers College, Columbia University: privately printed, 1949.
2. Small, L. A., Sweat, L. G., and Von Arnold, B., "Personality Needs as Determinants of Vocational Choice and Their Relationship to School and Work Achievement." New York Vocational Advisory Service, 1955.
3. Super, Donald E., *The Psychology of Careers*. New York: Harper and Brothers, 1957.

FRANK B. WOMER
University of Michigan

Using Tests

● This title, "Using Tests," is a very good one. It could let me talk about almost anything! But let us discuss a few important principles about testing under four general headings: *Why* should we test, *What* should we test, *How* should testing be *organized*, and *How* should test results be *interpreted*? The discussion will have to be brief, not covering all the factors. Naturally, we will be talking about standardized tests, not teacher-made classroom tests.

Why Test?

We test to secure information, of a normative type, that may be useful in decision making. This is to secure information potentially useful to us or to our counselees. By normative type, we mean information from a standardized test that tells us how the individual stands on the test in relation to the group used in the normative group. Thus a reading test normed for college freshmen tells us which are the best readers, which are average, and which are the slowest readers. Standardized tests help us rank people in order, without giving us information about specific knowledge or skills at a given level. We must remember this distinction.

We certainly give tests to improve counselee insights, so he can gain more information about his own skills, abilities, interests, and personality characteristics. This enables him to develop better understanding of his own desires and feelings, his own general personality.

Tests are also given to help counselors develop insights about their counselees. We may also give tests to stimulate counseling, e.g. simply to give us something to talk about. The mere talking about test results with the counselee may have as much benefit as the results themselves. It may simply be an entree to get started. The test results may eventually fade out of the picture. This is all right and still can be an important use of testing.

Selection and/or placement are other important uses of testing. However, these are of less specific importance in counseling and guidance situations.

What Should Be Tested?

There are four general areas here. First, we test *abilities*. Let us here define "ability" very broadly as "being able to profit from a college education." This means the student has those skills, knowledges, and understandings to go into a classroom and do the tasks he is expected to do. This is a *developed* ability and we are not concerned whether we inherit it or acquire it, i.e., where it comes from.

Some of the specific tests used to give us this type of information are the:

> *Scholastic Aptitude Test* (College Board)
> *Preliminary Aptitude Test* (College Board)
> *ACT Test Battery* (American College Testing Program)
> *NMSQT* (National Merit Scholarship Program)
> *School and College Ability Test* (Educational Testing Service)
> *Differential Aptitude Tests* (Psychological Corporation)
> *College Qualification Test* (Psychological Corporation)

Many of these, tests of generalized ability, highly verbal in nature, are actually given before the student arrives in college. The secondary schools are thus helping us get much of this information we formerly had to acquire for ourselves.

Next is the area of *achievement*. Here we find such tests as these:

> *Achievement Series* of the College Board
> *ACT Battery* (should be listed here, too)
> *Advanced Placement Tests* (College Board)
> *Sequential Tests of Educational Progress* (Educational Testing Service)
> *Purdue Reading Test* (Purdue University)
> *Nelson-Denny Reading Test* (Houghton Mifflin)

The achievement category is just slightly removed from the ability category. The two fall along a continuum, with achievement tests oriented somewhat more toward the outcomes of specific instruction than are ability tests. All of them are really related to outcomes of instruction, and the distinction between ability and achievement is often hard to define.

Another general area of tests is the whole area of *interest* tests, such as:

> *Strong Vocational Interest Blank* (Stanford University)
> *Minnesota Vocational Interest Inventory* (Psychological Corporation)
> *Opinion, Attitude and Interest Survey* (OAIS Testing Program, Ann Arbor, Michigan)

There is also the whole area of *personality* testing where perhaps, in terms of group use, the most widely used is the *Minnesota Multiphasic Personality Inventory*. The *OAIS* may also fit in here. There are, too, various "incomplete sentences" tests. We could list here the individually administered tests used by clinical psychologists (e.g., Rorschach, TAT), though they may be used less in educational-vocational guidance.

I don't wish to go into great detail about any of the tests we have listed. But I will mention a recent new reference in which you might be interested. This is something additional to the Buros series of *Mental Measurements Yearbooks*. Educational Testing Service has just now published a much smaller volume, *Bibliography of Tests for Junior and Community College Use*. There is no similar reference just for four-year colleges. This pulls together test names and a short description of all tests that might be used in the freshman and sophomore years. It is cross-indexed with Buros, so you can locate test reviews. The above title is approximate, I can't give it exactly, but the author is Dean Seibel, and it is issued by the Advisory and Evaluation Office of E.T.S. This should help you locate it.

How Should Testing Be Organized?

First, there is test information needed for all students: the test information that happens to be already available on records, and the test information needed for individual students. The first type includes the ability and achievement tests needed for placement or selection. Much of this may already be available on the high school record for most students and so there is much reduction in the general freshman testing program at many colleges. We should concentrate on tests that may fill gaps in students' records.

Above and beyond the general tests for everyone, I suggest you develop an extensive test library, having a package or two of many different tests for supplemental use with individual students. Interest inventories, for example, would probably be better here than using them hit or miss with all students. Many times we can do a much better job of not wasting the time of large groups of students by tailoring our testing to the individual needs of specific individual cases.

How Test Results Should Be Interpreted

In a counseling situation it is generally best to talk to the counselee *before* you do the testing. It is better to get acquainted, make him feel at ease, and get him to talk about his goals, interests, and so forth before you look at test results. I would tend to go to the test file after one has had at least one initial interview with the counselee. Then see whether the test record seems to confirm the opinions you have gained from the interview. Many times they will, sometimes they don't. If they don't, there is certainly the need for some additional thought on your part, possibly some additional testing. The fact then may be a difference between your opinion and the test results. This doesn't necessarily mean the tests are wrong; it may not mean you are wrong either. It just means there is some difference in information that has to be reconciled in some fashion. Then it is logical to consider if additional testing is necessary or would be beneficial.

After additional testing, if this is done, or the next time the counselee comes around, it is very important to get the counselee's opinion or feeling in relation to the test results. Too often we assume there are specific interpretations of test scores that automatically apply to all counselees. This simply is not true. We miss an awful lot of information if we don't ask counselees themselves to interpret, think about, or react to the test scores that they have produced for us. They are the ones that took the test; in general, they are more familiar with the items in the test unless you are extremely conscientious and regularly go through the test item by item—which I doubt most of us do. Thus the counselees have much more of a feeling for what is in the test. It is a great waste of information to ignore, in fact not to seek out, their reaction to the test scores.

In college situations it is very important to consider the use of *local* norms whenever possible, whenever feasible. College student populations vary so much from institution to institution that general norms, national norms, even regional norms many times simply do not apply to a specific given institution. So I would strongly urge that for any test you use on any large number of your students you gather information to develop your own norms just as rapidly as possible. Don't wait till you get one thousand or five thousand cases; start out with whatever you have and develop temporary norms and add to these and alter them as more information is acquired.

In looking at test scores I think it is very important to look for two things, a patterning of scores and any specific variations in that pattern. By and large the first thing I look for is whether there is any *consistent* pattern. Is this counselee consistently falling at the high scores, or consistently at the middle, or consistently at low scores? If this consistency is found in this counselee over a period of years or on a number of different tests, one can then have considerable confidence that this is his typical functioning level. Notice I did not say maximum functioning level. On the other hand, whenever you find some great aberrations, some scores high and some scores low, this simply indicates the counselee's performance has been erratic. It doesn't tell you why it was erratic, but it does identify the fact that sometimes he has been able to do much better than others. This calls for considerable concern on your part as to why this erratic pattern may have occurred.

Finally, I would hope that in the whole area of test use you would attempt to develop a "middle ground" in testing. Too often we go to the extremes. We either lean upon test scores too much and assume they are giving us exact, precise information, or else we say they are no good at all and ignore them. There is here a big middle ground that is the correct approach. Test results can give us *useful* information, but do not necessarily give us precise, exact information that is always true.

WILLIAM R. ROGERS
Earlham College

Mental Health Issues in Liberal Arts Colleges and Their Implications for Curricular Development

● While curricular development is most frequently geared to the methods and content of particular academic disciplines, this paper is an attempt to examine some general curricular proposals which derive, instead, from an analysis of four pervasive psychological problems that exist among college students. The four problems to be considered here will be those of anxiety, of dependency, of conformity, and of alienation. In each case the discussion will proceed from observations about these problems as experienced by students to some curricular suggestions that may help in their amelioration.

1. Anxiety

Anxiety is of course experienced in a wide variety of ways by college students. But there are several ways in which the learning disturbances associated with heightened anxiety are accentuated by the institutional and curricular structures themselves. To the general anxieties about adequacy in learning and competence in the examination system of the institution, good liberal arts colleges tend to add a subtle but destructively complicating factor in their implicit *rewarding of anxiety*. By this I mean that frequently the rewards of esteem from one's peers and concern and respect from the faculty are given when the student is anxious about his work, struggling with the subtleties of problems, depressed, over-worked, or caught up in the complexity of ambiguities about life and one's subject matter. The liberal arts college rewards such a person by regarding him as sophisticated, profound, and existential, and tends to judge those who are able to have fun as being superficial, to judge those who are calm or relaxed about their work as being uninvolved, or to judge those who feel on top of their studies as being too facile in their observations and short-circuited in their reading. Under such circumstances, it pays to be anxious, unfulfilled, or even depressed about one's work. Yet under such conditions it is obviously difficult for the person really to achieve genuine sophistication or a profound understanding of the subject matter.

In order to encourage the psychologically healthy alternation between work and relaxation necessary to learning, it is particularly crucial that good liberal arts colleges find some ways of rewarding either activity or ease not bound by the intensity of academic struggle. I think the academic faculty can, without betraying their allegiance to the tasks of the intellect, encourage free times of enjoyment and abandon with students, relaxed times in faculty homes, on ski trips or excursions to cultural events, in eating together, or in other ways. Special funds have been made available to Earlham faculty this year to encourage just such occasions.

We also need to work with teaching faculty to help them develop pedagogical procedures that will be sensitive to the anxiety level of students. The teachers' willingness to be known as persons, to be open, to be receptive and empathic to where the students really are in their own learning and growth, would do a great deal toward reducing the general anxiety in the classroom. It would be possible, for instance, to have some intensive workshops with faculty members in which problems of this sort were dealt with and in which various models of response to the questions and concerns of students could be acted out and discussed.

Insofar as the curricular structure creates anxiety through its internal examination or evaluation system, another possibility would be more extended use of outside examiners. When a professor who has taught a course later stands over his students in judgment about what they have learned, inevitable discontinuity results. But if the professor were able to stand with his students in the learning process as a colleague, stimulator, and catalyst evoking their growth as well as his own, the context of learning might be considerably improved. Some colleges have developed special funds for instituting this kind of practice and make regular use of outside examiners from other colleges to assess the progress made in a course.

Still another curricular innovation which relates to reduction of anxiety is the institution of a pass-fail grading system rather than a five- or eleven-point grading system of A, A-, B, etc. Under such a system, students feel more free to investigate material at their own pace and to move in directions that are fulfilling to them, without having to face the competition and anxiety that sometimes result, particularly when one is taking a course in a field outside his own major discipline.

A general contributing cause of student anxiety, broader than the curricular or examination system itself, is undoubtedly the perpetual ambivalence that the American educational system has between permissiveness and intense competition. In numerous ways we tell our students that they have freedom to investigate problems with which they are concerned, to develop internally regulated rather than externally enforced discipline, to elect among a wide range of courses and faculty members, to make, change, and re-make the pattern of their major area of concentration; and yet subtly in the background is the fierce competition for placement in graduate school, business, or government, and the general competitive ethos of the American capitalistic economy. In the educational system, competition probably emerges most strikingly in a student's experience of examinations. In this context, it seems crucial that clear expectations be made well in advance of examinations so that within this general structure the permissiveness and freedom that a student is given can be utilized realistically in relation to the necessary work that is required to meet the competitive demands. The clarity of such expectations seems especially crucial at points of general comprehensive examination where the student is required to integrate work either from the introductory sequences or at the senior comprehensive level. Confusion, misunderstanding, or vagueness about the requirements of such broad examinations are especially anxiety-producing.

Undoubtedly the largest single source of anxiety among students at this time is the conflict in Vietnam and the demands of the Selective Service System. Not only are students anxious about our national foreign policy and military involvement in itself, but also the stringent eventuality of the draft cuts off the normal possibility for students who might wish to leave school for a period of time to work, or reflect, or clarify their sense of identity. Freedom to pull back in this way to examine the course of one's life without immediate academic pressures is extremely crucial in the careers of many creative persons. But under the present conditions, it is relatively impossible for a young man to take such an option when things become confusing or immobile for him in the college environment. In this connection, the liberal arts colleges should vigorously pursue the possibility of establishing a *five-year degree program*. A five-year program could be instituted in such a way that considerable flexibility for a year off-campus might be insured for those who wished to take such an option. Such a program is agreeable with the Selective Service System as individual colleges give it an educational rationale and structure. And I believe it can be thoroughly justified both on educational and on psychological grounds. Without such a possibility, the sense of trappedness and helplessness that overcomes students when they see no viable alternative for their future can only be intensified with the resulting depression, listlessness, or revolt that we so often see as destructive ways of coping with this helplessness.

2. Dependency

Another psychological problem not unrelated to the ways in which one copes with anxiety is that of dependency. Here again, liberal arts colleges, often by virtue of the very strength of their sense of community and close faculty-student relationships, may be prone to sustain and reward a dependent relationship of the student on the professor and the institution. Furthermore, it may be rewarding to the professor to give unconscious encouragement to extensive dependency relationships on the part of some students, since this undoubtedly raises the professor's own sense of attractiveness, kindness, understanding, or knowledgeability. The warmth of personal encounter can too easily become a subtle manipulation of personal aggrandizement at the cost of the independence of the other.

To encourage greater independence, there are a number of curricular possibilities that may be employed. Here, again, such possibilities have both educational and psychological merit. A number of schools have already incorporated programs of independent study in which students undertake investigation of a problem of their own design and do a great deal of research in their own fashion, in conjunction with some faculty adviser. Also, foreign study programs have been adopted on a rather broad scale as a way of encouraging self-confidence and autonomous growth in a cultural setting that offers an intrinsic excitement of new approaches to learning as well as the opportunity for independent living. Foreign study programs that are overly paternalistic in either the course program or the control and centrality of their living arrangements may unwittingly void the opportunities for independent growth which occur when students have a responsibility for making their own living arrangements with families or other students, and for establishing some of the pattern of their own courses.

Two other curricular ideas have also come into practice in the past few years which encourage independence.

One idea is the possibility of freshmen seminars, in which a small group of eight or ten freshmen begin to work immediately with a professor on a research problem of a disciplinary or interdisciplinary nature. Such a seminar can help a freshman recognize something of what it is like to work on a frontier of a field study, to recognize problems of research design, to gain experience in group decision-making and the process of interpersonal sensitivity and leadership. It also, of course, breaks the pattern of traditional high school courses immediately. The range of content in these seminars in our experience has covered research in reconstructing paleo environments, critical problems on Homeric poems, problems in Scandinavian megalithic culture, R.N.A., and the problems of eugenics, economic, political, and geological problems in The Burns Ditch project, and so forth.

Another curricular experiment which pushes the possibility for independent work a bit further is a freshman and sophomore experience which at Earlham we term "Program II." In this program, open to any incoming freshman and elected by approximately a quarter of the class, the student joins a small tutorial group of eight to ten students meeting with a faculty tutor and two upper-class tutors. The tutor works with the students in arranging a flexible and individually oriented program of studies that meets each student's own pace and interests. The resources available include regular classes in the general college program, special Program II presentations and discussions of an interdisciplinary nature in various divisions, library book and tape recording holdings, and the tutorial group sessions themselves. Students are able with the help of the tutors to determine which resources best fit their way of studying and how the time allocation among these resources should be planned. No regular grade pattern or examinations are held in Program II until the student feels prepared at the end of the year to undertake a comprehensive examination testing his competence in the work that he has covered. Thus the emphasis is put on independent learning and integration of ideas, rather than on some lock-step system of course credits and grades. At points, this system may increase the anxiety of the students because of the uncertainty of expectations; but once individual patterns of study and research have been formulated through the regular individual and group discussions with the tutor, students develop a much clearer and more relevant idea about their education and a more stable internal pattern of motivation and discipline.

3. Conformity

Conformity may be viewed as one defensive method of coping with feelings of dependency and anxiety in a student's initial response to a new situation in the liberal arts college or elsewhere. Unfortunately, however, here again good liberal arts colleges somehow fall into the trap of institutionally encouraging conformity within the student body. Admission standards sometimes become so refined, either around SAT scores or other scales designed to identify the capable student, that a high degree of homogeneity results in the student body. Furthermore, diversity in the types of behavior, dress, and life perspective of the students may be distasteful to the administration of a college out of respect (or fear) for the public constituents and donors to the college. Conformity may also be implicitly reinforced through a Greek system, or, among those colleges which pride themselves on not having fraternities and sororities, in the more subtle but just as vicious in-group patterning of "jocks," "grubs," "hippies," or "intellectuals."

We know, of course, that such implicit or explicit homogeneity within a student body tends to cut off genuine expressions of individuality and innovation in establishing one's own life style. We also know, from Erikson and others, that to establish a mature sense of personal identity it is important to be able to go through a period of identity diffusion in which various models of behavior may be explored (1). To cut off such possibilities would be to cut off the range of opportunity for critical experience out of which a mature and well considered sense of identity might develop.

To insure heterogeneity in a student body, it would seem important that the admissions policy of a college be examined carefully so as not to restrict narrowly the types of students admitted along particular socio-economic and intellectual variables. Some schools have found it particularly helpful in this regard to have an active faculty admissions committee setting policy and even in some cases reviewing admissions folders.

The course structure itself can also be arranged to help counteract homogeneity and conformity. Nevitt Sanford has an interesting discussion of what he calls a challenge and response model (2). Using this model, courses are so arranged that the students have to encounter new situations either from case presentation or from actual experience in the community, which they cannot cope with using present value systems or information. They are stretched, in a sense, to have to begin by looking at other possibilities for understanding the situation and to respond creatively. To work, for instance, with the political, economic, and moral problems involved in desegregating housing, or to work with the ethical and medical problems in the loss of civil rights on entering a mental hospital, one has to develop new strategies and new points of view which bring him out of previously defensive or restrictive patterns of conformity.

Still another curricular measure for meeting this problem is the possibility of student exchange programs or foreign study programs. Exposure to student community life in other areas of our own country or in Asian, African, or European countries obviously expands the perspective of students in ways that break traditional patterns of looking at life, and encourage new and independent thinking. New possibilities in this regard have also been introduced with the increasing consortium arrangements of liberal arts colleges and universities. It may be possible for productive exchanges to occur here which will aid both the academic work of the student and his exposure to greater varieties of meaning and style in life.

4. Alienation

Alienation, while on one level polar to conformity, may on another level be an expression of conformity to various dissident and rebellious activities against all forms of external structure. Unfortunately, of course, the forms which alienation takes in protests, riots, demonstrations, dress, and behavior are sometimes so effective on college administrations that we lose sight of the possibility of communicating with the students and attempting to understand the real meaning and intention of their rebellion. I am personally convinced that if we do listen to this we can learn a good many important things that we should know both about educational institutions and our culture. And, furthermore, we can understand this alienation as an important dimension of a genuine education process. This is to suggest that while some alienation may be simply a matter of conformity, a great deal of it is rather a product of very thoughtful and sensitive reflection on various forms of corruption, dehumanization, and materialism in our culture that men ought to be objecting to and morally alienated from.

I am suggesting that what looks like defiant, dirty, or immoral activity may, in fact, be a radical outcry concealing a smouldering but legitimate protest against all forms of hypocrisy within our educational and cultural system—against the injustice of allowing some men an education and not others; against a pretence at values of honesty and reliability covering deceitful and manipulative business and educational practices; against easy liberal speech about integration which conceals self-righteous and self-protective insulation from real interaction with minority groups; against a destructive war conducted in the name of peace, and a forced conscription system controlling a young man's destiny conducted in the name of freedom.

One direct curricular way of meeting problems of alienation is to give a seminar in alienation itself. This could be an integrated seminar, drawing on literary, political, philosophical, sociological, or psychological material. Earlham is conducting such a seminar this winter, drawing in people who have given considerable thought to this—Graham Blaine at Harvard, Seymour Halleck at the University of Wisconsin, and Jean Shepherd from New York—but mainly organized so that students can investigate both their own experience and contemporary mass media regarding the roots of student alienation and despair.

Another sort of course which can do something similar would be a seminar in situational ethics, in which one started with the real ethical dilemmas of college students and developed discussion of ethical principles out of this genuine experience as well as from the more classical ethical theorists.

Work-study programs could also provide greater opportunity for students to be engaged in a real situation in which they have some possibility of acting creatively and overcoming the sense of impotence which clutches at some of their sterile sense of irrelevancy in a normal curricular pattern.

Another project that can be carried on within the local area of the liberal arts college might be social service laboratories or social change laboratories, in which students spend some time either in a service agency of the community or in working with some project attempting social change, but do so in consultation with faculty members capable of enriching the educational experience through discussion of the problems of human relations, leadership, decision-making, public opinion changes, political constraints, socioeconomic variables, and the like.

Crucial to the institution's way of meeting problems of alienation is the student-faculty advising relationship. Perhaps "advising" is a misnomer, for what I have in mind is the necessary on-going, open, sensitive relationships between faculty members and students in which students are free to explore their existential concerns and to work them through in personally relevant ways. It may be that workshops are needed for faculty advisers, to aid them in developing such sensitivity and keenness of perception, getting models of various types of response to student concerns and the implications they carry.

In spite of creative attempts to deal with the problem of alienation within the institution and curricular structure, it is clear that the problem runs much deeper. Liberal arts colleges, like all institutions in our culture, are caught in a climate of frustration and helplessness about international tensions and our involvement in domestic and foreign policy which is increasingly reaching crisis proportions. The extent to which hostility and rebellion is increasing among students only reflects a broader cultural feeling of impotence and frustration about national policies which seem to be ambiguous, ineffective, and crushing to the spirit of real freedom and independence among the young men and women of our nation. Until these broader cultural problems can be met effectively and real social change can come about, the effectiveness of any institutional policies, no matter how creative, will be severely limited. I personally applaud the program under way to unite private liberal arts colleges into a politically effective unit that can focus attention on some of these national problems in ways that will express vigorously the experience of men and women who can no longer concentrate on academic studies or on problems of personal growth when they feel trapped and helpless in a system in which they feel little personal control but rather an overwhelming sense of a forced destiny of life and death proportions.

REFERENCES

1. Erikson, Erik, *Identity and the Life Cycle*. New York: International Universities Press, 1958.
2. Sanford, Nevitt, *Self and Society*. New York: Atherton Press, 1966.

PANEL PRESENTATION

INNOVATIONS AND NEW DIRECTIONS IN COUNSELING

HERBERT I. POSIN, M.D.
Brandeis University

Philosophy and Trends

● A useful way to understand the present and to scan the future is to see how we got to where we are today. In order to discuss current innovations and new trends in college counseling, I would like to begin with a brief view of our past history.

I suppose college counseling and guidance began the first time a student went to a teacher for advice or help in a matter that had nothing to do with academic learning or a specific discipline. It is only relatively recently that the concept of guidance, counseling, or college mental health has taken on the aspect of a field *suis generis*, rather than the natural action of a younger troubled person seeking out the help of an older, wiser, trusted one. Perhaps something has been lost in this change, but this basic ingredient remains. College student counseling has developed into an area of knowledge and practice because a pertinent body of supporting scientific information has come into being and because it has gradually become more apparent that things are not always what they seem. These two converging influences have brought us where we are today.

As the study of a person unique to himself developed into a field of psychology, the concept of psychological testing grew and produced a battery of test instruments. These were supposed to give an objective, scientific evaluation of the subject's mental capacities, personality traits, aptitudes, and interests. Since many students came to helpers with problems of study difficulties or educational and vocational choice problems, these instruments met existing needs. The development of this special field of psychology, and the appearance of people skilled in the field and interested in college students and their problems, gave rise to formal organizations generally called counseling centers.

With the development of knowledge and interest in depth psychology, it became clear that things are not always what they seem. Sometimes students couldn't seem to apply commonsense solutions to their problems. They came with problems which were not translatable into questions or propositions which formal psychological tests could answer. The dynamic psychological principles first presented by Freud, his followers, and their dissidents presented new ways in which to view students' problems. A new value judgment crept in—the idea of encouraging the student to seek self-determination, autonomy, and responsibility for himself, encouragement to face personal problems and to make his own decisions. This shifted the whole technical and stylistic approach from that of "Here is the word!" to an attempt to get the student to explore his feelings, motivations, doubts, and fears. And this in turn required a staff which was not only acquainted with the theories of dynamic depth psychology but had learned the new style of the one-to-one interview situation.

As medicine began to recognize psychiatry as a legitimate member of its family, student health services became interested in obtaining the help of consultant psychiatrists. As best I can discover, the first full-time college psychiatrist was appointed to the United States Military Academy in the late nineteenth century as part of the military medical establishment; but incorporating the psychiatrist into the college student health program has lagged far behind the development of student health programs in general. Even now the majority of college and university health services have either no psychiatrist at all or use a psychiatrist only for consultation in acute emergencies. The presence of a psychiatrist as a member of the student health service has not been entirely a boon, however. An educational institution which would employ a psychiatrist in a meaningful way usually already had a well developed counseling center of some type, staffed by psychologists. Under these circumstances there was great potential for friction, misunderstanding, competition, and hostility, and unfortunately this potential was too often realized. More than personality clashes, hurt feelings, and professional jealousies were involved; there was often a serious philosophical difference of opinion. The counselors saw their work as semi-educational and did not tend to think of their clients as sick, while the psychiatrist operated within the medical model and might use the label "sick" or "not sick" and think in terms of "therapy" rather than "education, guidance, or counseling." This difference of outlook was partially bridged and partially widened by the introduction of the concepts of Erik Erikson with his formulation of psycho-social stages of development and maturity and his concept of identity crisis, which has unfortunately now become corrupted to a cliché. Is the psycho-social sanctuary which college provides an accidental structuring of our society, or is it something that each adolescent is entitled to? And does his use of college as a sanctuary indicate sickness, health, or something not related to sickness or health?

At present, there is a great variety of structural forms which college counseling centers can take. Among these are: (1) a solitary member of the psychology department who is interested; (2) the college chaplain who is drafted; (3) a formal organization of psychologists not related to the student health department; (4) an organization in which a group of psychiatrists and psychologists function as an integral part of the student health service. This does not exhaust all the variations. Any of these formats may or may not also include career or vocational counseling.

Where are we going? To some degree this will be determined by the uses the students and the university make of us. In this regard we share the present dilemma of the American university at large. Our higher educational institutions are under pressure from the society which supports them to train and prepare students to fill needed and important places in that society. The students often see the university as a place where they would like to have their own needs for knowledge fulfilled, but the students' ideas of what is pertinent and relevant knowledge are not always identical with those of society or the faculty or the administration. They drive towards a goal expressed in various ways—"self-actualization," "self-knowledge," "full emotional experiencing," "commitment," and often including rejection of many of society's values. This drive can be a valid means of intellectual and personal growth, but it can also be a means of rebellion, of avoiding outer reality problems, or a way of dealing with inner anxieties and drives. Therefore, many of the students whom we see will be difficult to categorize in the concept of sick or not sick, except perhaps by evaluating the degree of impairment of function. The tensions between the concepts and protagonists of sick–not sick, medical–non-medical will be heightened. Students themselves are confused about whether to think of themselves as "sick." These tensions and uncertainties will be reflected in our administrative attitudes and policies in such matters as the keeping of records and whether or not to include them with medical records. We will have to decide on a policy of communication with the university administration, government agencies, graduate schools, etc. If we decide our students are "sick," there is an existing medical model of handling these matters. If we decide we are helping our students to "learn" or "grow," then we have an educational model to follow.

In recent years we have seen renewed interest in the study of the interaction of social forces and the individual. It is hard to maintain emotional and mental equilibrium in situations of great flux and uncertainty—which is the climate of our time. Also, it is evident that students vary in ego and drive organization. They are confronted with different types of university attitudes and policies, with different campus climates, and with different viewpoints, demands, and expectations from various faculty and administrative personnel. We should identify the significant matches and mis-matches between the educational and administrative practices and policies on one hand, and the ego and drive organization of the individual on the other. Ideally, this should require colleges to undergo constant self-scrutiny, and the use of instruments to measure learning and thinking styles of students, so that better fit may be obtained. This might well be a whole new area in which the counseling centers could be involved.

There will be great demand on us to give our veto or imprimatur to various means of handling problems which really arise out of changes in social values, ethics, customs, and usage. How should the university deal with the change in the student's attitude toward sexual activity and drugs? Although one may find mental health aspects to many administrative decisions, we need to keep clear in our own minds that we do not have the last word on many issues. I feel we must resist pressure to speak as authorities on issues which are not in our professional area of expertise, but in which we do have informed personal opinions. In areas of ethics and morals, I believe we speak only as educated and thoughtful members of society who ourselves are struggling (more or less) with these issues. However, we can and should be helpful to the administration by helping it to think through and clarify its feelings, concerns, and goals, so that its decisions on these matters will be as rational as possible. I believe there is a healthy trend for some counseling centers to meet regularly with groups of administrators or faculty, not for therapeutic purposes but to foster their understanding of the emotional components of the issues existing on the campus.

I believe that our future activities, therefore, will take two courses, but not in divergent directions. One path will continue in the tradition of the past, that of helping the individual student deal with his intrapsychic and interpersonal problems. The other path will lead to a sophisticated psycho-sociological study of the particular college society and its interaction with the student.

MILTON R. CUDNEY
Western Michigan University

The Use of Immediacy in Counseling

● One of the goals of counseling is to change a person's behavior so that in the long haul he can live more effectively and productively than before. Some research results indicate that we have not been too successful in achieving this goal (2). In this paper I would like to suggest that a greater impact on behavior can result by recognizing and utilizing the dynamics of the counseling encounter itself. A skilled counselor can work with his client in such a way that the dynamics of the immediate encounter become apparent to both, and then use this interaction so that the client becomes aware of his behavior as it develops.

Historically, counseling has focused on problems. The problems may have been educational, vocational, or personal-social, but the focus is usually on something outside the immediate interaction between counselor and client. In fact, most clients fail to see this interaction as bearing on their problems. They must learn to look at their relationship with the counselor as something that is potentially valuable to their growth. Much counseling, too, focuses on past events and the importance of case histories, test data, and information about the family. This can be helpful, of course, but it often results in the belief by people approaching counseling that by delving into the past and understanding it, somehow all their problems will be solved. This does not often result, and too frequently clients can honestly say, after reviewing their pasts, "I understand all that, but I still can't do anything about my difficulties." Other counseling approaches, instead of dealing with history, concern themselves with present-day problems of the client. But this is not necessarily dealing with immediacy if the focus is away from what is going on in the client's immediate experiencing of life—at that moment, with the counselor himself. Dealing with immediacy is an exploratory running awareness of life as it is lived.

The Adlerians seem to realize the importance of focusing on immediate behavior. They believe that man's main desire is to "belong" and that a focus on how he is attempting to find his place is important. Going back into the past is done only to see what conclusions can be drawn from it. They believe only the consequences of past behavior can be known. The cause of behavior is not very important, partly because so often the cause can never be known, and partly because there are multiple causes for any one particular kind of behavior. Dreikurs, the leading Adlerian spokesman, suggests that we show the client how he is using a particular form of behavior and what he is getting out of its perpetuation. This can be done effectively if the client is brought to realize what particular behavior he is using in the counseling situation itself, and what he hopes to gain from it.

Kell and Mueller (5, p. 9) stress the importance of the counselor being aware of the various forms and intensities of eliciting behaviors that clients use in the counseling situation. They have found "that eliciting behaviors occur immediately in a counseling relationship and continue in one form or another throughout the relationship." Clients perpetuate behavior in their interpersonal relationships that actually impede the building of satisfactory relationships. For the counselor to focus on these kinds of behavior in a face-to-face relationship, in a manner in which the client does not feel a need to defend himself, is one means of helping the client change.

Glasser (4, p. 46) compares reality therapy with conventional therapy. He says, "Conventional psychiatry, almost without fail, relates this cause [of a problem] to instances in his previous life when the patient was unable to cope with stress. . . . Our job is to help the patient help himself to fulfill his needs right now. . . . Treatment, therefore, is not to give him understanding of past misfortunes which caused his 'illness,' but to help him to function in a better way right now." Reality therapists are not as interested in the past as in one's present functioning and in getting people to behave in the way reality would seem to dictate.

Berne (1) has described various kinds of "games" people play which interfere with a straightforward relationship of one person with another. They are a kind of interceding behavior which is not called for by the encounter but is brought to bear on the encounter for a perceived need on the part of one of the people involved. Many reasons can be cited to explain the maintenance of games in relationships. The explanation of an obvious one goes something like this: A child was faced with some frustrating situations in interactions with significant people—usually his parents—in his early life. In reacting to these people he discovered that by playing a "game" he seemed to get along better with them—they accepted him more, or praised him, or paid attention to him. He became less frustrated. Having worked once, he tried the "game" again with equally satisfying results. He behaved similarly over and over again until it patterned his approach to many kinds of interactions. Now he takes the game into relationships not because it realistically fits the situation, but because he was successful with it in the past.

Existential philosophy has contributed an understanding to counselors of the necessity of experiencing in the moment, and the importance of being aware of the moment. Farson (3, p. 15) in a statement typical of the existential counselor, says, "An important lesson for me has been to realize that the big moments in a relationship often come when I can allow myself to be vulnerable—when I can permit the possibility of change in myself. I seem to be able to do this infrequently, but it usually happens when I can risk being transparently genuine about my own immediate reactions."

A dissatisfaction with kinds of counseling that over-emphasizes the importance of understanding the past, or deals with abstractions outside of counseling, has moved many people to try to find more productive ways of counseling. It seems to me that the work of Dreikurs, Kell and Mueller, Glasser, and many existentialist counselors has opened the way for other counselors to see the importance of using the direct counseling relationship as grist for the counseling mill. It might come to pass that a student would come to a counselor not merely to solve a particular educational problem, but in addition to try to build up a relationship, work out the obstacles to the relationship, and learn more productive ways of relating to people. Or he might conceivably just go to a counselor to relate for the value of relating. Farson puts it this way: "We must learn to value counseling for what it does best—and what it can do is to provide an experience in humanness."

When a client comes to a counselor, he brings with him those ways of relating that he has learned in the past. His relationships with significant people in his early years, most notably his parents and siblings, have made a great impact on what he is like today. He has gotten used to his behaviors and found them to be in some degree effective. In other ways his behaviors may not be effective, but he is confused about what to do about them because he does not see them very clearly and does not know how to go about finding ways of replacing old behaviors. Often his fears of relinquishing the familiar get in the way of finding the new. Thus, when the client sees the counselor for the first time he relates in ways he has learned. The way he relates with the counselor is a snapshot of the way he relates with others. And because the behavior is alive rather than over and done, changes can occur. Decisions can be made today to change immediate behavior, if the client can become aware of his behavior and these decision points. The following examples illustrate the use of immediacy in counseling.

One client cautiously approached the topic of sex with the counselor. The counselor did not respond to what was said about sex, but to how the client approached the topic with him, and this opened the door to her confused feelings about sex and her relationship with her mother. It also illustrated to her how she projected feelings she had about her mother onto other people and, because of these projections, had to deal with others in unrealistic ways.

A young male student requested to see a female counselor. Scheduling made this difficult, so he ended up with a man. He presented himself to the counselor, vague, polite, tongue tied. The counselor reacted to the way he presented himself, delving into why the relationship had been entered into as it was. Eventually it became known to both client and counselor that relationships with men were particularly difficult for this young man because he saw all older men somewhat as he saw his father, from whom he constantly expected rejection, especially if he appeared weak. He had not been able to speak to the counselor because he had fought against looking bad.

A client talked on and on. Both counselor and client became bored. The counselor reacted to his own boredom and elicited the client's assistance in trying to figure out why they were relating in such a manner that they were bored. They found that the client controlled people by talking—about anything. In counseling, she controlled the situation by talking about things that really did not matter that much to her; she kept herself out of what she said because it was safer that way. A focus on this provided both the counselor and the client with a way for looking deeper into the client and her approach to life.

A person may have learned that dependency evoked favorable responses in the family, but now, as a college student, dependency evokes rejection from others. He is confused. He comes to the counselor. He comes, though, trying to establish a dependency relationship with the counselor. If the two of them get caught up in talking about the client rather than about the reasons behind the client's behavior with the counselor, the real issue is missed.

Counselors who try to deal with immediacy may find that it can be rather threatening, for it is not just the client's behavior that makes up the immediate encounter. An analysis of the present interaction may suggest needed changes in the counselor's behavior. But for those who deal in immediacy there is an aliveness and excitement in counseling that is often lacking in going over problems in history. Counselors can deal more with life in the making, can find themselves in on crucial decisions people make, can find themselves standing next to a person after wading through a plethora of resistances, can find themselves liking their job much more. I imagine the feeling a counselor experiences in dealing with immediacy is akin to that of a scientist when he discovers something exciting in the laboratory, or a writer when things fall creatively into place.

Clients come to counseling manipulating, hostile, rejecting, testing. They invest or do not invest; they are afraid; they present weakness; they attempt to seduce; they stay in a shell; they hide; they try to force the counselor to be responsible; they try to force punishment from the counselor; they apologize for being human. If the counseling does not focus on trying to understand these things, growth possibilities for clients can be missed.

A Theory of Behavior Supporting the Use of Immediacy

Each of us accumulates a variety of experiences as we tread our way through life, and we use these past experiences to assist us in coping with present situations. We rely on the past to direct us in the future. Past experiences fall into patterns: some people may call them habits, or structures of personality, or categories of reacting. These structures determine much of our behavior. Our behavior is determined by these past experiences, however, only to the extent that we are unaware of the way we perpetuate these patterns. We cannot change the past, but by being aware of our constant immediate choices we can decide the degree to which we allow the past to dictate our present behavior. This is to say that many of the difficulties in which we find ourselves as humans, we bring upon ourselves by the choices we make.

Unfortunately, too many people are unaware of the choices they make. They are made in the realm of the unconscious. For instance, a person who is dependent makes constant choices every day that keeps him dependent. The person who fails when he has plenty of ability to succeed makes choices that bring on failure. It boils down to this: A person coming to a particular encounter with life, counseling included, does not come fresh. He comes with a burden of categories and structures that prevent his experiencing reality except as it is screened through these past experiences. He can either allow this to continue, or he can make choices that will diminish the influence his past has on him.

Techniques for Dealing with Immediacy

People seek counseling for a variety of reasons. If the counselor believes he can help his client most by dealing with immediacy, it may be appropriate for him to explain the importance, as he sees it, of taking a look at the immediate client-counselor interaction. This can be helpful in eliciting client co-operation. In addition, if the client can see the benefits of being aware of his behavior as it happens in counseling, he might become aware of the importance of behavior outside of the counseling office, and decisions he did not know he had might become more available to him. Rather than blame a particular behavior on something out of his control, for instance, the client might catch himself making decisions he never knew he had been making.

Often behavior manifests itself in counseling, which the counselor is unable to identify explicitly. There can be many reasons for this—counselor defenses, lack of training, limited understanding of personality development, the client has given only part of the picture, or unawareness of such things as manipulation by the client. Yet the counselor can sense that the relationship is stalled, that he is bored, that he is in a bind with the client, that the client seems to put restrictions on him, that he is being punished, that the client is afraid and stands away from him, or that the client leaves the movement of counseling entirely up to the counselor. Here again, eliciting the client's co-operation in understanding what is going on can be helpful. He may have data that the counselor does not have, and if it is shared it may illuminate that which has not been seen. Having the client actively working in counseling can produce many benefits. At a termination session after fifteen appointments, a client once said to me, "You know, I've done most of the work in here. You haven't really done that much." I answered, "That's true. And you probably have grown to the extent that you have worked."

In counseling, clients often talk about their relationships with others. It is not unreasonable to suppose that many times it is the client's way of saying something to the counselor about the client-counselor relationship. Because the counselor is a significant "other" to the client, it behooves him to ask, when the client talks about how he relates with others, "How does this fit into our relationship?" The counselor needs to be aware of, and to take advantage of, ways he can open the way for an exploration of his relationship with the client as one means of assisting the client to improve his relationships with others.

Undoubtedly the most productive way of helping the client recognize the importance of the immediate relationship as a means of growth for himself is through counselor openness. Counselors too often fear that their own openness will wreck the relationship, but surprisingly enough it most often works the other way around. Counselor openness might bring into the open something both are vaguely aware of and is a hindrance to movement, and this would clear the path to an exploration of it. I would like to suggest that in most cases counselors are not open with their clients because of their own fears, rather than for the clients' benefit as, unfortunately, they often believe. I say "unfortunately," because if the counselor recognized that he was limiting his openness out of his own fears, he would be more likely to see his fears for what they were and to work through them.

To blame or threaten the client for the way he is behaving in counseling would destroy the use of immediacy in counseling. If the counselor can approach the client's behavior, as well as his own, in a way that indicates his interest in understanding their dynamics for the benefits that would result, if he deals with the data as he would with any meaningful data, and does not attach to behavior such things as blame or judgment which come out of his own limitations as a person, he will see an increased ability of the client to deal with immediacy.

Bringing About the Actual Behavior Change

Much of my interaction with people in counseling involves, as this paper suggests, living in the immediate situation with the client. First, I want us to get a fairly realistic feel for the behavior being manifested in the session. Identifying patterns of reacting and the ways a person transfers to the counselor are examples of this. I try to help him see how he keeps these behaviors intact by the choices he makes, and help him see that there are other choices that, if selected, might result in greater happiness.

Because I am working for the individual, I suggest to him that a place to begin making changes is in the situation with me. So we take a look at that. When he may have kept me in the image of a parent and now chooses to see me more as I really am, when he may have been fearful of me and now realizes that fear does not belong in the live encounter but was brought in from some place else, when he may have hidden himself out of fear of rejection but quits hiding with me—then behavior changes are starting to occur. To really assure behavior changes, the client must go out of the counseling situation with a willingness to try making different choices in his everyday life. But as he makes different choices with me, I try to give him honest feedback about the impact they have on me. It is of utmost importance that the client get this honest feedback. He assumed neurotic behavior because he didn't get candid reaction in the first place, and if, as he makes a choice to risk change, we do not "give it to him straight," we may well drive him back into himself.

Fortunately, what happens to me as people make new choices for themselves—choices other than those that produced ineffective or destructive behavior—is that I love them more, find myself excited about our relationship, share more of myself. Sometimes I find it difficult to contain my joy for the person who decides, for example, to feel for me, when before to feel was too frightening. I don't react for effect or because I think this is what they need. Clients know somewhere inside themselves if the counselor is playing the reinforcement game and is manipulating them for particular ends, and then they will resist change. Change is assured when a client decides to make decisions other than those he has made in the past and then finds that people react more favorably towards him, or that his job goes better now, or that the stomach cramps leave. Thus, he is convinced that to make choices other than the ones he made before is valuable, and the patterns of behavior he carried with him are discarded for others that work better.

In summary, let me say that I do not believe dealing with immediacy is the only answer to helping clients grow. It must be utilized as it fits the client's unique life situation. Once when Victor Frankel was lecturing on logotherapy someone asked, "Is logotherapy the only thing you do to help the people who come to you?" He answered no, it was helpful to about 20 per cent of the people he saw; with the other 80 per cent, he used other psychiatric techniques. That's how I feel about dealing with immediacy. The counselor who can successfully use it has one more means with which he can help clients who come to him for his services.

REFERENCES

1. Berne, Eric, *Games People Play*. New York: Grove Press, Inc., 1964.
2. Eysenck, Hans J., "The Effects of Psychotherapy: An Evaluation." *Journal of Consulting Psychology*, 1952, *16*, 319-324.
3. Farson, Richard E., "What Are People For?" in Wayne R. Maes (ed.), *The Elementary School Counselor: A Venture in Humanness*. Tempe: Arizona State University, College of Education.
4. Glasser, William, *Reality Therapy*. New York: Harper and Row, 1965.
5. Kell, Bill L., and Mueller, William J., *Impact and Change: A Study of Counseling Relationships*. New York: Appleton-Century-Crofts, 1966.

WESTON H. MORRILL
ALLEN E. IVEY
EUGENE R. OETTING
Colorado State University

The College Counseling Center:
A Center for Student Development

● Colorado State University's Counseling Center is changing its entire orientation in a major attempt to create a new model for mental health intervention on the college campus. Three basic directions for program planning guide these changes. Two of these directions grow out of modern trends in community mental health: movement out into the community, creating programs based on primary prevention rather than remediation; and mobilization of community resources for mental health. The third is a new definition for the role of the counselor and of the counseling service based on a developmental rather than a counseling or therapeutic framework.

Counseling centers, for the most part, have been isolated from the academic and living environments of the campus. Counseling staff members have tended to wait for students to come to them for help and have been able to offer assistance or intervention only after a problem has emerged. The concept of the student development center, much like that of the community mental health center, requires that the counseling center staff become an active part of the university environment, interacting with administration, faculty, and students to create changes that lead to maximum growth and development in all groups. The counseling staff must do more than counsel; it must also try to mobilize community resources by providing consultation and assistance to individuals throughout the campus community who are in a position to help others deal with the problems that occur. In short, the counseling center staff should be involved in helping prevent the causes of mental disturbance and should mobilize the total campus community as a mental health resource.

We have found that working with a campus community suggests the need for a new conceptual framework for mental health. The developmental framework described by Oetting (6) has been especially helpful: a mental health problem is defined very broadly as anything that interferes with or prevents the use of the developmental tasks that are available in the environment for personal growth. Treatment planning is based on a behavioral diagnosis. We try to see what behavior is missing in the client or the environment and endeavor to teach new ways of behaving and meeting situations or attempt to change the environment. The major effect of this change has been to question seriously the validity of providing the same treatment, whether "relationship counseling" or "therapy" or "vocational guidance," to everyone who enters the center. The concept has also led us to design entirely new kinds of treatment programs, attempting to create meaningful and valuable developmental tasks for individuals who need them in order to benefit from the environment in which they find themselves.

The developmental model also emphasizes the greatest potential for growth by providing programs which facilitate and enhance the development of the "normal" student, one who cannot be described as having developmental inadequacies. Thus, the role of the counseling center is broadened to include the development and growth of all students, rather than only those who have a problem or block that must be overcome.

The following sections describe some new programs. Some have already been started, others are still in the planning stage. Together they point toward a new kind of campus institution, the center for student development. Within such a center, service, training, and research would be integrated into an ongoing and continually changing program for mental health intervention on the campus.

Planning for Innovation

The counseling center, as a center for student development, is designed to provide for the planning, implementation, and evaluation of programs aimed at meeting the mental health needs on a college campus. The center is an integral part of the campus, serving as a catalyst for educational change, bringing faculty and students together in meaningful encounters, and changing and growing itself as the environment changes. It is planned to modify itself continually in response to informational feedback. It is a laboratory where innovations can be tested in a practical setting and where their impact on students and institutions can be assessed.

The following programs are aimed at creating a climate for change on the campus, increasing encounters between campus populations, and dealing with the individual problems of students. First are the basic groups organizing and maintaining the process of change.

The Evaluation Team—An Internal Feedback Mechanism

In order to determine the effectiveness of programs and their application to student and institutional needs, any overall plan must provide for evaluation. This has typically meant some kind of external assessment of whether an individual or organization is functioning effectively and meeting its goals. The Evaluation Team is, instead, an integral part of the ongoing process of change within a counseling service. It should not be an external source of criticism, but an internal mechanism for providing feedback to the counseling center staff, allowing it to plan for greater effectiveness.

Whether a service is attempting to create innovative programs or simply provide a high level of traditional service, it should be constantly evaluating its programs and their impact. The Evaluation Team consists of staff members with interests and skills in research design and instrumentation, who are assigned the responsibility of assisting the staff members in judging the effectiveness of their efforts. It serves to 1) provide knowledge of results to the counseling staff, 2) provide for the dissemination and publication of findings to the community of individuals and agencies concerned with the problems of mental health on campus, and 3) serve as the agent of continual change in the structure of the counseling service.

To provide this kind of service, an evaluation plan of some kind should be prepared for every new or ongoing program. The plan should be worked out with the staff who will be involved in the program, and the actual responsibility for evaluation should be given to that staff. While there may be some loss in objectivity when staff is simultaneously involved in programming and in evaluation, there is a corresponding increase in involvement of the staff in the evaluation process, and a far greater chance that the requisite data will actually be obtained. The Evaluation Team serves as consultants, developing an overall evaluation plan with the staff involved, helping with data collection, analysis, and in the preparation of reports.

Research in applied settings places a number of limitations on evaluation. First, care must be taken to secure the willing co-operation of the project's service personnel, who may be prone to feel that evaluation and research are being imposed upon them and that the requirements of evaluation may interfere with the service they are providing. This problem may be partially overcome by involving service personnel in the planning and conduct of evaluation as well as by providing informational feedback which will serve to illustrate the value of evaluation in the improvement of service. For the same reason, tests and other instrumentation must be kept relatively short and must either have a high face validity to the personnel administering them or must be explained and discussed carefully so that they feel that they are engaged in a worthwhile activity in filling them out.

Another problem is that of developing adequate control comparisons. In the press of service and consultation demands, random numbers and control groups have a way of evaporating. Because of this, considerable ingenuity must be exercised in the design of project evaluation; this design must yield useful information and at the same time cause minimal interference with ongoing center operations.

Along the same lines, the counseling center can serve as an internal feedback mechanism for the university. It can provide valuable information for administration use in program planning. Too often, a university administration feels that there is little understanding of its problems by faculty, students, or the usual counseling staff. The administrator in the university is frequently viewed as the enemy by students and by faculty. He is the one who has to be fought for whatever change is being sought at the moment. He is the one who does not provide enough money, or enough space, or will not change or ignore a regulation to meet an immediate need. Neither students nor faculty are usually willing to acknowledge the problems that the administrator faces: the limited facilities and funds available for everyone's needs; the attitudes of the legislators that must be considered in obtaining funds; the longer viewpoint and the need to consider cost to the institution if a change should fail. The counseling center should, to the best of its ability, assist the administration in its planning and in its day to day operations by providing a constant flow of relevant information.

The Student Development Planning Team

The Student Development Planning Team will be responsible for studying the impact of the university on the student and identifying those factors which influence his growth and development. The team will be headed by the director of the center and will include a sociologist or anthropologist to initiate studies of the campus ecology both independently and under the direction of the Planning Team. The team will also include representatives from the student body as well as members of the faculty selected for their concern with student development and their ability to communicate with the other faculty. The plans also include the formation of a voluntary student-faculty committee to work with the Planning Team. This committee would include the dean of students, student leaders, and other faculty members selected for their interest and ability to contribute various viewpoints to the discussion. It may shift membership frequently and will contribute to changing the set of the Planning Team as well as providing valuable communication with the faculty and students.

The Planning Team will have two functions. One of these would be to provide a groundwork of theoretical knowledge and information about student development that could be fed back to the counseling center to aid in program planning. This would include seeking and providing information about the developmental level of students and the developmental skills involved in the growth process. Description of the ecology and environment of the campus should perhaps be the primary agenda of the Planning Team. There could be, however, a secondary agenda of communicating new attitudes to the faculty. The faculty on the voluntary committee would provide the strongest channel of communication with the community at large.

A Crisis Projection Team

A Crisis Projection Team will be concerned with studying the potential crises that can occur on a campus. These can range from a "Texas Tower" incident to a "sit in" in a dean's office protesting or demanding something. Clearly, some kinds of crises, such as murder or suicide, should be prevented to whatever extent is possible. These can range from recommending planting of shrubs around high rise buildings (a recommended procedure for reducing attractiveness to potential suicides) to developing thorough plans for dealing with a student standing on top of such a building. This team would also be concerned with recommending programs for early identification of such problems, so that in some cases, at least, early intervention might lead to prevention of the crisis.

Some other crises, such as the "sit in," rarely need prevention, but unless they are predicted and there is previous planning, they can lead to unfortunate situations that are damaging to all concerned. The team could also be concerned with this kind of situation and work out tentative plans and alternatives that appear to have the best potential for leading to personal growth instead of damage. A key aspect of such planning is a clear understanding that individuals and the university can actually benefit from crises. The girl having an anxiety attack in the residence hall can, if treated inappropriately, actually become severely "mentally ill"; and other girls in the hall can feel highly threatened and fearful and develop other problems because of the incident. Dealing with the situation in appropriate ways, on the other hand, can make the crisis a meaningful experience in the girl's development, and can lead to growth in those others whose lives touch on the crisis (2). Thus, the Crisis Projection Team has two primary roles: to prevent crisis and to exploit crisis when it does occur.

Student Advisory Developmental Groups

Student Advisory Developmental Groups will provide a constant contact with and feedback from students, which will be crucial for providing information to the center. Groups of volunteer students will be selected to meet for a given quarter as advisory groups for the center. Their discussions will center around their needs, their own development, and the role that the university plays in hindering or assisting that development. These students will provide a constant source of new data on the college "scene," leading to new programs and new processes of innovation in center programs. This data could also be fed back to the university faculty and administration as information about the changing needs and activities of students. This provides one more contact point for an encounter between faculty and student groups and places the center in a position to monitor that encounter and plan programs to effectively increase it. Kennedy (4), at Kansas State, is using a similar program with great effect.

Another major goal of the Student Advisory Developmental Groups would be the change in the students themselves. The student discussing his own development and the factors that influence it must become more aware of the developmental process, the environmental factors that effect it, and his own potential for using these factors in effective ways. Olsen (7), at Lawrence, has successfully used similar programs.

Plans also include the employment of a Student Advisor in the center on a half-time basis while he attends college. He would be a junior or senior with a range of experience in student affairs and with the ability to communicate on a personal level with student leaders. His primary function would be to serve as consultant to the staff of the center.

Faculty Advisory Developmental Program

Associated with the above, a Faculty Advisory Developmental Program will provide for increased faculty involvement in the function of the counseling center as well as providing effective communication between the center and other faculty. A small group of faculty will be asked to serve as advisors to the counseling center on student developmental needs. A faculty member will meet with one of the Student Advisory Developmental Groups as a consultant, and then meet with a staff member of the center to summarize his impressions of the students and their developmental needs. Kennedy (4) has used a program like this with great success.

A major purpose of the program would be to obtain information, not only about the students, but about faculty attitudes. This could also be an important learning experience for the faculty member, since it places him in a position where he must listen to students discussing their needs and their own development. The member of the center staff conferring with the faculty member also has the opportunity to teach techniques of helping students express themselves clearly and openly, and to suggest new roles for the faculty member to play in the group in order to further communication, as well as new approaches and new techniques for him to use in working with students.

The use of faculty members as counselors is another program designed both to create new ideas within the center and to modify faculty attitudes and skills. The counseling center plans to employ a small number of teaching faculty in the center on a part-time basis. These faculty will be selected for their interest and capability, and will be asked to bring their special knowledge of their disciplines to bear in creating new and valuable roles for the counseling center as a center for student development.

Workers in student personnel have traditionally tended to isolate themselves from the faculty, and have thereby removed themselves from a valuable source of creative ideas. Under this plan, the faculty members would function within the center in appropriate roles. They would be encouraged to involve themselves in whatever functions they would like to try: counseling, study help, serving as group leaders, working with the educational encounter programs of the center, or innovating new programs of their own.

At a minimum, this group should provide the center with valuable variety in experience and background. At its best, the faculty counselors could become a really creative force and learn attitudes and skills within the center that they will bring to their entire future careers as professors.

Programming for Student Development

Stress Conferences: Education with Encounter

Stress Conferences, modeled on the national programs, provide a means of establishing fruitful student-faculty encounters. Conferences of this nature will be planned by the Planning Team and will involve student leaders, selected faculty, and the center staff. While the present emphasis on stress provides a meaningful conference topic at the moment, there are other issues that can serve as the content core of a conference. As the center develops, this kind of conference could be expanded to include an almost continuous program of relatively unstructured conferences on useful topics. The series of conferences should help in developing a model for programming that can utilize any meaningful topic as a base and yield a maximum of information and interpersonal encounter. Among the questions still to be answered are: How much structure is necessary? When should programs be structured and when open? Should groups be relatively homogeneous or disparate? What are the characteristics of faculty that lead to successful exchanges between them and students?

This kind of conference is relatively new. It is neither a group dynamics nor T-group experience, nor is it a structured program designed for information dissemination. It is, instead, a model for the basic concept of encounter. Faculty, students, and the center staff are all expected to bring their own viewpoints to the encounter, and the situation must provide a chance for expression of these viewpoints. At the same time, the conference must create an environment in which a viewpoint is respected and each person is willing and eager to grasp the other's point of view as well as to express his own. The focus is on intellect *and* feeling, interpersonal respect *and* interpersonal communication. A great deal of concern has been expressed over the "generation gap." Within this concept, there is no great attempt to reduce this gap. In fact, the growth of our society requires a continual gap. Without trying to change the values of the faculty to those of the new generation, or the attitudes of the new generation back to those of the older one, we can create a meaningful encounter between the two, leaving both with respect for, and some understanding of, the other.

Developmental Counseling

The medical and rehabilitation model of repair to a "norm" is probably an outmoded concept of counseling. The developmental approach provides a new basis for counseling center programs aimed at dealing with individuals who are unable to use the college experience for personal growth and development. This developmental approach does not mean that all traditional counseling concepts are dismissed. Individual counseling, group therapy, occupational and educational information, and other programs are all relevant to the developmental concept. However, these programs have in the past been too oriented to problem solving, rehabilitation, and remediation. Counseling must be more developmental in nature. We should not counsel students to solve problems, but should counsel them in such a way that they learn the techniques involved in problem solving.

As an example, vocational counseling has been concerned with the traditional concepts of vocational choice and career decision. This kind of counseling might have been appropriate in a culture that provided stable occupations, with apprenticeship leading to journeyman and finally master status, where the skills of the master would solve all of the problems that his vocation could present. We no longer live in that kind of society. Today, occupations develop, grow to maturity, and become obsolescent with such speed that the learning of a single set of skills may lead to unemployment within a decade. The older techniques of test interpretation, choosing a major, and planning a career actually can lead to a distorted view of the occupational process. Today we frequently find young men in their thirties requesting vocational counseling. They are reasonably successful, enjoying much of their occupational life, but are concerned about whether they have made the *right* decision. They are afraid that, if they become much older, they will be unable to change their minds. This idea that occupations are rigid domains, and that if you make the right decision everything will be stable and secure and satisfying, derives from previous concepts of occupational choice, beginning with asking, at an early age, "What are you going to be when you grow up?" The process of vocational counseling should create in the student, not the idea that he must choose an occupation, but that he faces a series of developmental tasks extending indefinitely into the future that will demand continual decisions and growth and the development of new skills and abilities (3).

In similar ways, study counseling should lead to development of new skills and the ability to continue learning new skills, and therapy for personal problems should be oriented not toward solving the problem, but toward long-term continuing personal growth. One of the tasks of the counseling center should be to develop new counseling techniques for creating this kind of process.

Media Therapy

Traditional techniques of treatment, such as analytic therapy and relationship therapy, are developmental tasks in themselves that may be necessary for dealing with individual problems of some students. The Center for Student Development will provide these forms of treatment when they appear to be meaningful in terms of the problem and the student. There are new approaches, however, that should be tested, and the center should be constantly seeking and evaluating these techniques. Among them are the possibilities offered by new techniques in videotape recording. The facilities of the present center include part-time use of two Ampex VR 7000 videotape recorders, including cameras and monitor units. Recent experience with videotape processes has presented us with an unparalleled opportunity for planning new forms of intervention in mental health. Our studies at this point suggest that a basic dimension in effective interpersonal encounter is *attending* behavior. Attending behavior seems to be characteristic of good counselors, and of individuals who are able to relate well to others. We have found that with videotape we can teach attending behavior to beginning counselors, students, and even secretarial personnel. It consists of certain immediate skills, such as maintaining appropriate eye contact between individuals and using a comfortable, natural posture with natural gestures. The other skills involve interpersonal process and are complex, but they can be taught as well. These are *following* what the other person has said, both intellectually and emotionally, and responding appropriately in words and feelings to his communications.

We have also done some preliminary work with videotape in dealing with interpersonal conflicts. For example, two roommates from a residence hall who were having some difficulties in their relationship were provided with some specific training in how to communicate with and understand each other. They talked with each other before the camera and then viewed their encounter along with a counselor who consulted with them about their ways of relating. The counselor trained them in some of the attending concepts, using immediate feedback from the video recording. This preliminary exploration indicates that the counselor can work effectively in this model in helping students with their interactional patterns. It appears that the counselor as a consultant can promote tremendous changes in the ability of two clients to interact on a meaningful level. New methods of individual and group treatment utilizing the counselor in the consultant model may greatly enhance the effectiveness of the counselor.

Television has been used as a medium for education, but primarily only to present the same kinds of content and in the same way they were presented without television. In training in attending behavior, we are using videotape in a completely new way, using its full impact for involvement. This may be the basic reason why the approach has such immediate and intense impact. Even listening to oneself on audio-tape somehow leads to a sense of isolation, and it is easy to deal only with the content of the tape. Seeing and hearing oneself interact with another, and having the aspects of that interaction called to your attention, is an intense, immediate, and involving experience.

The use of this approach for training counselors is highly important. There are other possibilities, however, that need to be explored. One of the most obvious is the effect of providing the developmental task of learning attending behavior to those students who have inadequate social relations and social skills. This kind of training would fit exceptionally well into the developmental counseling framework. Other possibilities include training students in therapy in attending behavior, and involving them in diads or groups with each other as well as with the therapist. A possibly more important program would be to train students in attending behavior in relation to their classwork and professors. Imagine the impact for educational change if students started paying close attention to what their professor is and what he says. It might even force the professor into paying attention to his students!

This is only the beginning of the exploration of media therapy. There are obvious parallels between the description of attending behavior and Rogers' necessary and sufficient conditions for psychotherapy. The therapist, in relationship therapy, is an involving and involved medium. In a sense, the person is the message. Ultimately, we may have to deal with this level of experience in terms of developmental tasks, but the potential for the use of the video media is only beginning to be tapped. One of the major tasks of the Center for Student Development will be to explore its assets and limitations.

Educational Change and Media Treatment

Educational TV on the college campus has not used the potential of the medium for involvement. It has been used primarily as a duplicating machine for lecturers. Observation of the students in a TV class suggests that they respond in the same way. Some watch and take notes, others fall into a trance, doodle, or doze. Where we have used videotape in ways that engage its capacity for involvement, we get a high level of absorption and interest.

Allowing the instructor to view himself lecturing is an obvious beginning, and the Audio-Visual service is doing this. Another possibility is to extend the model to a small group of students, taping them and recording by split screen the professor and his lecture, then playing the tape back and asking the students to comment on their reactions as feedback to the lecturer. The medium itself, when used for feedback, seems to demand attention to process. As exploration continues, the students and faculty themselves will undoubtedly contribute new ideas and new concepts to be tested.

Campus Consultation Programs

One of the major activities of the center will be consultation with all kinds of campus groups. Moving outside of the walls of the center in this way has already proven to be an effective means for providing remedial programs, for early identification of severe problems, and for creating a climate for change.

This past year an especially successful program of consultation with dormitory head residents and student assistants was initiated. CSU has approximately 6,000 students in large campus residence halls and ranks in the top fifteen of American universities in number of students housed on campus. Instead of mere chats with residence halls requesting appropriate referrals, counseling center staff went out to the dormitories to serve as active consultants in a variety of ways according to the interests and skills of the consultant psychologist.

We found that psychologists were valuable in counseling in the dormitory setting itself, that they ran sensitivity groups that helped head residents and students communicate more effectively, that they provided more effective liaison between the counseling center and the residence hall, that they helped head residents communicate more directly with their staffs. A myriad of possibilities for communication were discovered. The psychologist as a consultant-facilitator proved to be a most popular role. The university is more and more seeing the role of the residence hall on campus as an important part of the educational experience rather than merely a custodial convenience.

Evaluation, Grading, and Tests: A Developmental Approach

A number of counseling centers score faculty tests, using such equipment as the Optical Scanning Reader. This usually includes item analysis and other special testing services. This service is useful to the faculty and offers greater involvement of the center in grading and evaluation. Examinations and evaluation are a major source of stress for both students and faculty. While it is clear that radical changes are needed in the basic concepts presently in effect, change will have to be slow, since massive tradition is involved. Center staff can begin to recommend procedures leading to better tests. The counseling center should provide consultation for the faculty member to help him develop better tests. With proper groundwork, it may be possible to help the faculty member ask questions such as, "What do I really want my students to learn?" "What kinds of evaluation would be really meaningful for that knowledge and for those skills?" "What kind of developmental tasks is my course offering that will lead to those changes?"

Among the other demands that students are making in asking to become involved in their own educational process is the demand for some involvement in their own evaluation. One of the early conferences developed by the center should lead to a significant encounter between faculty and students on the subject of grading and evaluation. At present, neither group understands or is willing to listen to the feelings of the other.

Psychometric and Automated Program Development

A psychometrist is available in many counseling centers for administering standard tests and psychometric measures related to evaluation. The center also plans to include an individual whose primary responsibility would be development of new psychometric instruments and techniques. Another staff member will be responsible for the development of automated programs providing meaningful developmental tasks for personal growth or for remediation of problems.

A primary use of tests in counseling has been the prediction of the success or failure of future alternatives. In using such tests, counselors can become simply prediction machines. In the context of developmental counseling, counselors must not be mechanical. They need to be concerned with identifying those developmental tasks that are needed by students in order for them to be successful. New tests are needed that, rather than merely predicting, will identify where a student falls in an overall developmental scale, and what kind of developmental tasks he needs in the future. Counselors need to recognize and accept the responsibility for facilitating the growth and development of the students in their charge. They must see that the student can use the developmental tasks in the educational environment for growth and development.

Standard tests have only borderline relevance to the developmental concept of counseling. Within academic content areas, we do have tests that assess development, but we badly need new concepts in testing for personal and social development. The developmental task aspect of taking tests should not be ignored in these studies. Taking a test can be a considerable learning experience if the test is properly developed. The center will also need instruments for evaluating and assessing outcome of innovative programs. Construction of psychometric instruments in the center will be a continuing and difficult job.

Programmed tests and programmed counseling have been successful adjuncts to the counseling process. Interpersonal interactions will not be replaced by such programs, but they can provide valuable developmental tasks for students, with little cost in staff time once they have been constructed (1, 5, 8). The labor involved in developing automated programs is immense, but some programs have already been constructed, and the reduced cost in staff time, once a successful program is devised, makes the effort worthwhile. The utilization level of such programs is also high, since they can generally be picked up for a new setting with only minor modification.

Consultants to the Counseling Center

The counseling center plans to enhance its programs by bringing a number of consultants into its operation to provide stimulation for new ideas and approaches to student development. Here too, however, a new role is projected for the consultant. Asking someone to come in, observe briefly, and then prepare a report on some aspect of operations seems to be a minimal way of involving a consultant in the operations of the counseling center, or of the university. There are some consultants whose time commitments may allow only this level of interaction, and whose opinions might seem valuable enough so that they would be used in this fashion. In general, however, the counseling center will try to use consultants in a new way. The consultant to the center, instead of being brought in for a period of only a day or two, will be hired for a period ranging from a week to a month. Consultant fees, under these circumstances, would not be at the maximal day rate, but would vary from somewhat more than a week's salary for the week-long period to the usual monthly salary of the individual spending a full month. The consultant, during this period, would be expected to actually run a program of some kind on the campus, providing a real service, and, at the same time, providing an opportunity for working as part of the staff of the center. The kind of program would depend on the particular skills and background of the consultant.

Training

Mental health, from the developmental point of view, is largely a training process. Even the engagements of therapy between the therapist and the patient can be seen as developmental tasks that provide training for the student involved. Within this framework, the consistent approach to training is that of providing meaningful and appropriate developmental tasks for the graduate students and interns involved. Identifying a series of developmental tasks, ranging from role playing through actual individual and group treatment, will be the first step in providing a meaningful model for training and supervision.

THE COUNSELOR—A HUMAN DEVELOPMENT CONSULTANT

An essential change in the role of the counselor is evident in the programs described. The counselor can no longer view himself as working within the confines of his office with individual students or groups of students with problems. He must become a human development consultant. As such, his effectiveness in providing meaningful service for the total college may be greatly enhanced. He must also begin to evaluate his role from the framework of mental health defined as the ability to engage in and utilize developmental tasks for future personal growth. As such, the university counselor will become the monitor for the entire educational process, intervening to maximize the student's potential for physiological, intellectual, social, and emotional growth.

REFERENCES

1. Berlin, J. I., and Wyckoff, L. B., *General Relationship Improvement Program.* Atlanta, Ga.: Human Development Institute, Inc., 1964.
2. Frick, W. B., "Adjustment vs. Growth: The College Student in Crisis" (mimeographed by author). Presented at Hope College Spring Workshop: Mental Health of College Students, April, 1967.
3. Ivey, A. E., and Morrill, W. H., "Career Process: A New Concept for Vocational Behavior." *Personnel and Guidance Journal*, in press.
4. Kennedy, K., Personal communication. Kansas State University, Lawrence, Kans., 1966.
5. Magoon, T., "Innovations in Counseling." *Journal of Counseling Psychology*, 11, No. 4:342-347 (1964).
6. Oetting, E. R., "Developmental Definition of Counseling Psychology." *Journal of Counseling Psychology*, 14 No. 4:382-385 (1967).
7. Olsen, E. H., "Innovations in Counseling." Symposium presented at the American Personnel and Guidance Association convention, Dallas, Texas, March, 1967.
8. Tiedeman, D. V., "Some Prospects for the Computer in Educational Research." Symposium presented at the AEDS-AERA session on Educational Research, Detroit, Mich., May, 1967.

Editor's Note:
   This paper, written by the three authors, was presented in briefer form at the Symposium by Dr. Morrill.

AARON L. RUTLEDGE
Merrill-Palmer Institute

A Systematic Approach to Pre-Marital Counseling

● Marriage today is supposed to combine the virtues of a vacation in a tropical paradise, a successful psychoanalysis, and a religious conversion experience, all in one painless dose. Educational efforts of both religion and social science, coupled with popular communication media, have raised the expectations from marriage to an all-time high. This is seen in the kinds of personality desired in a mate, as well as in what is expected of him socially, economically, in the love life, and in terms of "happiness." Yet there are many barriers to marital preparedness. Emotional infantilism, unconscious ambivalent needs, re-enactment of early unsatisfactory relationships, the push of sex and loneliness, lack of other avenues to symbolic adulthood, all coupled with a pollyanna promise of self-fulfillment in all these areas can add up to an irresistible push toward the altar. Such a ground swell can leave little time or energy for pre-marital counseling.

The trouble is that "know how" has failed to keep pace with the rising goals for marital success. It is like being convinced of the pot of gold at the end of the rainbow, only to find the end is out of reach, or like offering the child candy on a shelf only to withhold the stepping stool which would make it possible to reach the sweets. When these high expectations are not forthcoming in a marriage, the result is alienation and misery. The couple is torn apart inwardly as they visualize the satisfactions desired in contrast to their present static marital state. It is little wonder that many give up in despair and find divorce necessary.

Readiness for Change

Much of the success of a marriage arrives ready-made in the

structure of the two personalities. But this is not as fatalistic as it might seem, since each mate also brings the possibility of change. Each person grows the basic timbers of personality in the early years of life. It is equally true, however, that one of the lasting characteristics of personality is the ability to change and grow.

A good proportion of marriages occur during adolescence, a time of personality upheaval. For youth in this culture, the degree of personality disorganization and confusion can have many of the earmarks of a pre-psychotic state, as the transition from childhood to adulthood, prolonged unmercifully in the absence of "rites of passage," activates any previous doubts about self. This is accompanied by activation of past hurts, excavation of painful memories, and the kind of confusion about self-identity and worth that can make adolescence a painful period indeed. To the healthier youth this state of "flux" provides an opportunity for reintegration of personality at a more meaningful level as he steps over into adulthood. For those who have been seriously deprived and crippled, or who do not receive sufficient guidance and assistance, the pain of the experience has to be guarded against, accounting for much of the bizarre acting-out behavior common to adolescence. The denial of the disturbing elements brought to awareness in the personality upheaval accounts for much of the stubborn refusal to accept professional help at this time.

There is something about an approaching wedding, at least for those who take the time to think at all about its seriousness, that can create the same state of individual upheaval common to adolescence. Popular humor about the insane nature of love is not without grounds. As thinking people of any age approach marriage, the emotional stage is set for personality change—regression, or stabilization by means of concretized personality defenses, or a new level of healthy integration setting the basis for continued growth—just as is true in the adolescent struggle. On the other hand, the activation of unresolved emotional needs, exacerbation of self doubts, dislodgment of defenses previously thought to be strengths, heightening of ambivalences, coupled with all the other anxiety-creating personality needs, can precipitate the drive into the marriage relationship. If means can be found to impinge upon the couple at the time of this upheaval, they can be helped to use the anxiety and energy from the turmoil as an investment in pre-marital counseling. The need is present, admitted or not. Someone must make them aware of the value and availability of professional assistance. Once the counselor is involved, the stimulus of engagement and aspirations for a good marriage can be utilized as an opportunity for renewed growth of both personality and relationship.

Every therapist knows how difficult it is to "tell" people the solution to problems or the secrets of growth. If the solution is only superimposed on old conditioning, it doesn't permeate their personalities, doesn't become integrated. It takes time to bring about personality change and renewed growth. Yet many young people will be particularly susceptible to guidance when approaching marriage, motivated by the emotional and sexual need for each other. The desire to establish a meaningful family life can be as strong as the need for sexual mating. Here is one of the "teachable moments" or opportunities for learning, the like of which comes only a few times after early childhood. A minimum of concentrated help here can bring about personality changes which might take years of psychotherapy to effect later.

"Delay marriage until you are more grown up," is a major plea, especially in middle-class groups, and the high rate of failure among early marriages justifies the admonition. But merely waiting for more birthdays may have little to do with maturing for marriage. College can be an extension of adolescence which gets in the way of the kind of emotional maturing necessary to marriage. The college youth thus, in effect, puts off for four years the kind of growing up and facing of adult responsibility which those who marry upon graduation from high school must begin to handle almost immediately, whether or not they are prepared.

At any age it is evident that immaturity is a primary cause of marital friction and breakdown, but little has been written about marriage as a positive force in growing up. The young engaged couple might be the first to admit their unreadiness for all responsibilities of "pair living" and parenthood. But it is as though all the forces for growth and health decide to cast their lot with marriage, knowing that it will call for and demand the best youth has, including continued growth. Along with the host of people who get hurt and end an early marriage, and those who have to "practice" in several marriages before being able to find one they can tolerate, the counselor must not lose sight of the tremendous challenge to growth which a marriage can provide. Such growth might never occur for some of those under the protective wings of the parental home.

This readiness for change in the engaged couple seems to be contradicted by the fact that most couples do not seek such help in getting ready for marriage. Such unwillingness may be based on ignorance of the value of counseling, or upon a sense of false modesty, or false pride. On the other hand, it may be fear of facing facts about oneself or about the relationship. Beneath the fears and hesitancy a genuine desire for assistance, which will assert itself once initial barriers are removed, often is found. The most frequent reason for not seeking help is the failure of homes, churches, schools, and counselors to underline its value and to make pre-marital counseling readily available. Increasingly, youth, particularly those who go to college, are seeking professional help to insure preparation for growth in their marriage, rather than risk hurt and failure.

Creative Use of the Engagement

The modern trend toward a formal engagement is society's way of preparing youth for the actual step into married living. All too often it is a blind-leading-the-blind game of brinksmanship. When properly understood, it offers an opportunity for correcting or learning to utilize those factors which make up both the strengths and inadequacies of the two personalities (4, p. 17). Herein lies the ideal opportunity for the pre-marital counselor.

The first task as the counselor works with the engaged couple is to help them examine their *total readiness* for marriage. Although they may have assumed such readiness, it is by no means assured. In the end they will decide when to marry, but the counselor is their guide and helper. The choices available are to get married just as they are in spite of the dangers, to break up a relationship that can only be unhealthy or soon end, or to set about in earnest getting ready for marriage with the counselor's aid.

Three areas of investigation claim the counselor's attention if he is to understand both people and to visualize them as a married pair: (1) Personality formation and feelings; (2) Role perception and attitudes of each about self and about the other; (3) Past failure or success in close personal relations. In this process each may come to a better understanding of self, of the prospective mate, and of the relationship they are growing. All such knowledge begins with the knowledge of self.

Things to Be Done

There are many areas related to personality development and to marriage relationship about which the young person needs to know as much as possible. Much of this knowledge has been attained in the process of growing up, but it needs to be corrected and supplemented by rigorous study of the marriage and family literature available. But facts are only the beginning of learning. The failure or success of a marriage seems to be more dependent upon attitudes and feelings and behavioral patterns than upon the knowledge of facts. Various specialists have estimated that 75 to 90 per cent of the factors involved in the meaningfulness of marriage are due to these less conscious, learned processes of relating and responding in close personal relationships.

(1) One of the foremost tasks of any young person who is contemplating marriage is the discovery of his basic selfhood and the *continued growth* of himself as a person; this is the first goal in premarital counseling. The kind of equalitarian marriage desired by increasing numbers of young people demands the highest level of maturity of those who undertake it. Although marriage itself can be a maturing process for an individual, he must have attained a reasonable degree of adult growth and responsibility if he is to carry his end of the multifaceted responsibilities of modern marriage.

(2) Perhaps *skill in communication* is as important as any other one factor in developing a healthy marriage. In spite of all of the modern media of communication in America and the almost overwhelming mass communication to which the citizenry is subjected, there is ample evidence that in more intimate relationships this is a nation of non-communicators. Early in development children are taught by example, if not by word of mouth, to conceal their real feelings about many things. All too often this is taken over to the dating stage by youth, basing their experience upon the "line" and upon a deceptive front. Dating and courtship catch young people at a period when egos are easily threatened. They are in the process of moving away from parents and yet have not proved themselves fully

as adults. If they have been reared to refuse to expose their inmost feelings lest they be hurt, then deception will play a major role in dating. A motto that seems to underlie much of this period of development is: "All's fair in love and war."

When two people enter into an engagement, or formally or informally begin thinking about marriage, the attitudes and techniques which are based upon deception and self-protection for the ego will be detrimental. A truce must be declared and time allowed for redefining roles and restructuring relationships to the end that they begin to understand each other and much of their own complicated make-up as individuals, and begin to evolve techniques for relating meaningfully together.

Without specific and deliberate intent to do otherwise, courtship and engagement may serve only as a continuation of subterfuge and camouflage of the basic personalities under a smokescreen of passionate love and as an opportunity for more intensive and exclusive rights to individual satisfaction. Social pressures are such that many status-conscious youth, although concluding separately or together that they might best break up, go into marriage because of familial and community expectations once the engagement has been announced. If there is real struggle within a relationship, a relationship which has meaning in spite of the conflict, there is a tendency to camouflage injured feelings and differences of opinion in order to maintain the delusion of complete agreement. To make this possible, often one of the couple develops a policy of giving in. This sets a pattern of smothering one personality and giving the other undue leeway in self-expression and a resultant false feeling of self-adequacy. This tends to turn into a missionary endeavor on the part of the more aggressive one to overhaul the personality of the yielding one.

Learning to communicate with honesty, sincerity, and intensity is one of the greatest means whereby the unmarried can prepare for a meaningful life in marriage. Attention will be given later to some of the many areas that call for this kind of careful communication.

(3) A third goal within the total process of preparation for marriage is that of *developing problem-solving skills*. This is part of the communication process. Communication skills are fundamental in this effort to face up to and try to resolve, or to accept as unsolvable, the many areas of difference that exist or might exist between a

couple. Much of the process of preparation for marriage is opening up these areas of life and projecting the young couple into the future, enabling them to visualize the kinds of problems they will have and, in many instances, to experience these now. With assistance, they can develop skills in handling the conflicts now, and these will become the basis of the additional skills necessary for handling these problems later in marriage.

Some Things Must Be Undone, Too

By the time people reach the age of marriage it is amazing how much of their daily living consists of fairly fixed patterns and habits. Much of this is healthy. Indeed, without habits there would not be enough energy to get through the day, what with all the decisions to be made about tying shoes, chewing food, combing hair, and perhaps even about kissing mother or wife goodbye on the way out to school or to work.

Nevertheless, there are many areas of habituated expression which can get in the way of intimate man-woman living in marriage. Part of the responsibility of a young couple preparing for marriage is to undo these conditionings and replace them with new forms of behavior that are less destructive and more promising of satisfaction within marriage. For instance, the man may have been conditioned from boyhood against feelings of tenderness, gentleness, and sweetness, and into a brusque, matter-of-fact aloofness that will leave a wife feeling unappreciated and unsatisfied. All too many men, and not a few women, become ill at ease and even embarrassed at the mention of these qualities which seem so necessary to success as lover and as parent. Parental and social expectations may have succeeded all too well in convincing the woman from girlhood that she does not have sexual feelings, or should not express them, or that it is the husband's responsibility to see that she is satisfied and a fault of his technique if she is not.

The process of preparing for marriage provides an opportunity for barriers to be melted, for people to learn to become spontaneous in these feelings which are fundamental to healthy marital relating. Likewise it is necessary to learn how to express hostile or hurtful feelings with each other without feeling any unusual threat to the relationship. Without learning how to handle the worst kinds of feeling it is inevitable that these will accumulate, and that efforts to control them will block out the more pleasant kinds of feelings. By learning to handle all kinds of feelings with each other, old patterns of responding can be ferreted out, understood, and laid aside as they are replaced by new patterns of responding and communicating.

In summary, the counselor's goals with the engaged couple are: (1) to test the growth and growth potential of each, (2) to stimulate and develop skills in spontaneous communication, and (3) to expose areas of stress and develop problem-solving skills. Either by individual or group contact he helps them face up to existing problems and those that can be anticipated. He can help them create an environment in which to clarify hindrances to growth and relating, to stimulate and capitalize upon feelings of adequacy, and to develop skills in relating and problem-solving which facilitate growth, both of the individuals and of the relationship. In this kind of relationship their love can continue to grow. A new family circle established by such efforts then becomes the nursery of a new generation of more competent marital partners.

If the engaged couple learns that this intense process unduly threatens their love for each other, if they cease to relate well and love fails to grow, the counselor can assist them in terminating their engagement with learning and health rather than hurt.

Why can't all of this be accomplished by the couple alone by studying all the facts of family living? Knowledge of facts is only one small part of readiness for marriage; attitudes, feelings, and learned patterns of responding are of much greater significance.

Along with the continued growth of each as a personality, and the development of communication and problem-solving skills, a couple must begin to gain the understandings of relating meaningfully in marriage. Relating within the affectional and sexual areas is not enough and, indeed, can camouflage the necessity for preparation within the many other areas that are just as vital to marriage. So much of the past has been closed off and has become unconscious that it is difficult indeed for young people to open up the many areas of life to the free kind of communication that is called for here. The more hurt there has been in particular areas of development, the more reticence to remember.

The primary purpose served by "content" or factual material—

whether in a textbook, in journal articles, films, or lectures—is to serve as a stimulus to remembering, to discussing with the counselor and the prospective mate, and to learning how to relate together around the reactions that follow. Counseling provides an opportunity to develop critical thinking and problem-solving skills as together the couple talks through their own feelings and reactions, with the counselor providing stimulus and guidance.

Since the "facts" of marriage vary from culture to culture, from social class to social class, religion to religion, country to city, and person to person, and since feelings and attitudes carry much greater weight in a marriage than does knowledge, the challenge is to help the couple open up the vital areas of life for intensive communication, long discussion, and a search for problem-solving skills as differences of opinion emerge between the couple.

Cultural patterns cannot only make people too sick for marriage; they can serve to make them well. One of the latter efforts is seen in the tradition of "engagement." This period provides a natural opportunity for correcting or learning to utilize many of those factors which make up both the strengths and inadequacies of the two personalities involved.

In putting together the experiences of hundreds of youths, along with family life educators, engagement is seen as providing an opportunity for:

(1) The total process of learning to understand and relate to each other in all circumstances. "I" and "you" become "we."

(2) Undoing unwholesome attitudes developed through earlier conditioning and dating experiences, and exploring the male-female likenesses and differences in general and as applicable to each couple.

(3) Understanding and evaluating each of the sets of parents, the parents' relationship to each other, the relationship of each to his parents, and the future relationship of the new family to the old family.

(4) Determining the kind of marriage and family life desired by each couple, and the beginning of thinking, feeling, and reacting in this context.

(5) The continuation of individual growth and acceptance of responsibility, in an atmosphere of love and appreciation, with the "push" of sexuality as one of the driving forces.

A Group Approach

Group counseling is beginning to hold its own with the individual method; indeed it can be the preferred method in preparation for marriage. There is a learning and healing potential within a group beyond that found in individual psychotherapy or counseling. A great variety of meaningful ways by which couples can relate, react, and respond can be elicited in the group so that the counselor does not have to assume a didactic role in most areas. Changes in thinking and feeling come about with group support that might be resisted if suggested directly by the counselor. Sometimes confused feelings or transference reactions can be examined with greater ease within a group than in the presence of just the fiance and the counselor, or of the counselor alone. Old hurts can be healed, the isolation of guilt can be broken, and fellowship restored with oneself and with others within an understanding group. The group can permit the individual to lose himself briefly if he must, but can also focus upon him or upon the couple's interaction if it is needed. Feelings of shyness, inadequacy, rebellion, or fear can be faced together, and be resolved or accepted, as each works out the riddle of being himself in a social milieu in an approaching marriage relationship (1, 2, 5).

Pre-marital counseling takes advantage of the natural heterosexual grouping of two people, moves it from relative isolation into a group of couples, which is a prototype of the larger community, where educative, re-educative, and corrective means of developing relationship competence can be brought to their assistance.

In setting up a group, criteria must be established for selecting any particular group of couples who will work together, whether it be availability or similarity or dissimilarity of such factors as age, education, religion, previous marital status, and emotional health. The engaged couples available at the moment, and the kind of group the marriage counselor prefers to work with, probably will be the primary determinants (1, chapt. VI, VII).

The author's text (4, chapt. V, VI) describes an approach that can be utilized with one couple or several, with illustrative case material. Such an approach has proved to be highly successful in leading to creative marriages, as well as a superior method of motivating youth to utilize counseling as an aid to personality growth.

A Brief Critique

Up to the present, most pre-marital counseling has been concentrated on the university campus. It tends to be associated with those courses which focus on the family and often represents an "over and beyond the call of duty" investment on the part of the instructor. To some extent this is equally true in those high schools where courses on the family are taught. University counseling centers tend to provide some pre-marital counseling, although the intensity and thoroughness with which it is done varies greatly. All too often pre-marital assistance is either strictly individual psychotherapy or superficial and didactic educational consultations with the engaged couple.

The author's own spot survey of individual clinicians—psychiatrists, psychologists, social workers, psychoanalysts, and marriage counselors—indicates that their experience in the pre-marital area is very much like that in other "preventive" practice. The clinician tends to talk a good line of prevention, but justifies his inactivity in those areas with cries of overload with disturbed people. No one doubts that there is an over-demand for treatment of disturbed individuals and marriages, but one is quickly led to believe that the promising field of pre-marital counseling is neglected by clinicians because it poses some unusual stresses and calls for continuous adaptation of the more typical unilateral therapeutic training. It runs counter to the now slowly changing psychoanalytic format of seeing only one patient, lest the transference be contaminated. Others have seen it running counter to the Rogerian devotion to one client to the exclusion of all other forces. It calls for an understanding of the dynamics of pair-interaction, that unique entity "the marriage," which is just now beginning to receive due attention. All of this is compounded by the almost total lack of specific training in pre-marital counseling in the graduate schools of the nation.

Historically, preparation for marriage has gone sometimes the education route and sometimes the clinical route, but usually the two procedures have gone hand in hand. Without belaboring the issue, research tends to indicate that those educational approaches that focus primarily upon facts, theories, and surveys tend to have little direct relationship to the actual functioning of marital interaction. On the other hand, those courses—certainly making use of research and other factual material—which operate along a functional line, incorporating therapeutic techniques, particularly when professional counseling is available as needed, do have a direct bearing upon the meaningfulness of future marital interaction. In terms of the long-term effects of intensive pre-marital counseling, whether with separate couples or groups of couples, the author has probably done as much specific work and made as much follow-up as almost anyone else. It is his conviction that this is where you beat the old "chicken and egg" dilemma. These chicks are highly motivated, once the ice is broken by professional contact, to utilize resources to develop the most meaningful marriage possible. They are the chickens that produce the new chicks that can represent a new generation of emotional and marital health.

If all clinicians would devote a fourth of their time to intensive pre-marital counseling, they could make a greater impact upon the health of this country than through all of their remaining activities combined. Particularly is it necessary to find a way to reach that part of the middle-class population which does not take the high school or college courses in the family area, and who, not suffering the grossest of neurosis, do not feel compelled to seek professional treatment. They need to be educated to the positive investment in marital health that is possible through pre-marital counseling. A crying need for family education in general and sex education in particular, not to mention specific pre-marital counseling, is coming from the population which seldom finishes high school or never goes to college. Here lie the greatest problems, the greatest challenge, and yet an infinitesimal amount of professional time is being focused upon these young marriages. This condition is only compounded when one turns to the "disadvantaged populations" that are at last receiving so much attention from other points of view today.

Only when specific and intensive training in pre-marital counseling becomes an integral part of the professional curriculum, only when adequate pre-marital counseling is made available to the professional himself while he is in training, planning to get married, or experiencing early marital stress—only when these two conditions are met will it become possible to have a substantial increase in the amount of professional pre-marital counseling.

REFERENCES

1. Bonner, Hubert, *Group Dynamics*. New York: The Ronald Press, 1959.
2. Moreno, Jacob L., *Psychodramatic Treatment of Marriage Problems*. New York: Beacon House, 1945.
3. Rutledge, Aaron L., "Individual and Marriage Counseling Inventory." Detroit: Merrill-Palmer Institute, 1956.
4. Rutledge, Aaron L., *Pre-Marital Counseling*. Cambridge: Schenkman Publishing Co., Inc., 1966.
5. Slavson, S. R., *The Field of Group Psychotherapy*. New York: International Universities Press, 1956.

TOPIC GROUP REPORTS

GROUP A

Development and Operation of a Counseling Service

Reported by HENRY GROMOLL, *Millikin University*

● One fact we noted was the wide range of counseling services found in the schools here represented. In the development of counseling programs on liberal arts campuses, we felt most of them are pretty much like Topsy—they just grew. We addressed ourselves to only a few of the main issues.

I. *Autonomy of the service:*

At the present time one of the obvious recommendations was the need for separation of disciplinary processes from the counseling function. The implementation of this separation varied broadly from institution to institution. One of the suggestions was to take a strong look at the kind of "title definitions" many of us have. Such titles as "counselor" or "dean" may tend either to facilitate or inhibit some of our functions.

II. *Voluntary nature of clientele:*

No general fast rule could be arrived at for a referral system other than the desirability of voluntary referrals. However, some of us recognized that in some instances involuntary referrals may be necessary. The real task here seemed to be essentially the concern that we should have about preparation for referral. The issue of voluntary or involuntary does not arise sharply when we consider how referrals are made from various sources. At least one of the tasks of the counselor, therefore, would be a need to have those others with whom he works learn how to make referrals. An involuntary referral might often be a matter of an inappropriate referral, or perhaps a referral that was poorly timed. Part of the referral process is indeed a counseling process, to prepare the student for acceptance of counseling activities.

III. *Confidentiality*

There was consensus on this point in the need for separation of counseling material and counseling files from personnel records. In discussing the problem of confidentiality, the issue of communication between referring sources and counselors came sharply into view. The observation was made that when confidentiality became almost a cult-like phenomenon on campus, this was usually due to poor networks of communication in which people functioned in a *title* capacity, relating not in terms of person-to-person, but of title-to-title. And underneath this, at least dynamically, was certainly some suspicion or lack of trust which impaired communication. Related to the issue of confidentiality was some caution we felt about communiques that occurred not only *within* the campus community, but communiques about clients *outside* the campus community. The observation, certainly a strong one, was made that often in the name of confidentiality we withhold information which could be helpful. This especially becomes an issue when personnel workers, within their own group, lack trust or communication.

IV. *Academic advising*

Academic advising is usually conceived as a separate function from that of counseling. In many instances there is certainly the need for co-ordination of effort. However, often we attempt to dump some of the counseling functions onto uninterested or overworked faculty. So we did not feel that an institution should fill the gap by utilizing faculty in direct counseling services; but the faculty could be helpful in terms of acquiring some of the listening skills, and supportive skills, that are consistent with good counseling and good referral practices.

V. *Fees*

Fee policies vary on different campuses, but usually when a

referral is made to an off-campus source the cost is considered the responsibility of the student. The student would have to underwrite the cost of out-patient psychotherapy, for example. One recommendation we would make to the symposium group would be the investigation of group insurance plans for those universities that could use consultative fees, consultative services, and/or diagnostic services of counselors or psychiatrists outside of the campus community. There are insurance plans that would cover some of the initial costs and provide quite directly some of the additional implementation through the counseling program.

VI. *Location*

We emphasized that the counseling services should be accessible to the student, but preferably away from an administrative organization if this appears to be a barrier to effective counseling. We felt that the typical counseling models should be reviewed to see if face-to-face consultation in someone's office is the only possible model to be considered. We felt that the "campus corner" counselor certainly was coming into his own, and that the counselor might consider activities *outside his office* as certainly in the province of good modern counseling technique. We were impressed with Dr. Morrill's presentation of wider utilization of counseling services, not only in a counseling center, but distributed to the dormitory setting, living arrangements, and other areas of the campus community. So, rather than choose between the individualized face-to-face approach versus a kind of community approach, we felt that both were potential sources of good counseling services.

VII. *Staff personnel*

Counseling, ideally, should be an integral part of the whole educational process. We felt that in many liberal arts colleges we really need to examine some of our present commitments to counseling programs, in terms of both budgetary and staffing considerations. The general observation was that many people in the counseling area wore too many hats—and I'm sure this expresses many problems in the liberal arts colleges. We would recommend a sincere and thoughtful consideration of just how important counseling is on a particular campus. Have we really made the kind of commitments we need to make? This was prompted by Professor Patterson's presentation. Counseling should, and does, go on at many levels of competence in a liberal arts institution—we indeed should not limit ourselves to narrow models. We felt that counseling was a Johnny-come-lately in many of our institutions; many of us felt that we were making do with essentially stop-gap tactics. To administrators and policy makers we suggest that our commitment to a counseling program should be examined. We also compared some of the differences between liberal arts schools and larger universities and colleges. As Professor Morrill pointed out, there were many problems of depersonalization in larger institutions, which were lacking on the smaller liberal arts campus. On the other hand, we felt that although we may have fewer depersonalization problems, another issue was the problem that some students have reflected to their counselors—that of "too much closeness" or "lack of privacy." This came out in many forms: "I feel everyone is watching me," "Our community is too tight a little community," "There are no ways in which one can seek a little alienation which would be necessary to the growth and development of our adolescence."

VIII. *Ethics*

We endorsed Dr. Jourard's person-centered approach rather than a mechanistic approach to counseling.

COMMENTS AND DISCUSSION

Question: You spoke of expanding the point of counseling outside of the office to other points. Do you mean the counselor should go to places and carry out informal contact, or what do you mean?

Answer: We were seeing the counselor as a consultant as well as a counselor, and to ignore the environmental stresses and strains when he could have at least some knowledge of them we felt was really wasting his potential skills. This going out of the office could involve consultation with faculty, administrators, groups of students in a dormitory, learning the physical characteristics of the environment, and the psychological characteristics of the environment as well. I don't think we were restricting ourselves.

Question: What about the size of the counseling staff? What might be considered an appropriate ratio of full-time counselors to student population?

Answer: We had no specific comments as to size of staff, but it is a good issue to address ourselves to. We were more concerned with the fact that the counseling service has grown like Topsy. In most institutions the ratio is certainly less than optimal.

Question: I have noticed a reluctance of faculty members to move very far into the counseling area because of their concern over how much of this is their legal right. This might be a topic to explore in the future.

Answer: I think much has been said about faculty-student relations with regard to freedom of disclosure and on what issues and when. I think our subcommittee recognizes the complexity of the issue of confidentiality, but we felt it became a sharp issue in interpersonal situations where trust was at stake or titles were at stake. I think there are some real legal issues on campus. Some professionals on campus are protected by law and others are not; they are definitely exposed.

Question: Apparently the majority are not. If a counselor happens to be a college chaplain there is protection of pastor confidentiality. If a counselor happens to be a history professor, it may be impossible for him to legally protect his confidentiality with the student.

Answer: Yes, this is true, if, for example, a faculty member, as opposed to a certified psychiatrist or psychologist, in confidence, was told by a student of the use of drugs. Yes, these should be issues of orientation or a new program when faculty members are used in some advising or counseling capacity. We should know and understand the laws of our state and where we stand. We need to carry this back and clarify this within our own institutions.

Question: Do you have the name of an insurance carrier for group insurance covering psychotherapy?

Answer: I can't give you a name offhand, but we could check it out. We have some bargaining power with carriers which we sometimes overlook, and there are many possibilities, such as a deductible plan. There are plans which will cover diagnostic services, and you could tailor these to cover the needs of your particular institution. It would be added implementation to services, e.g., if some student might have to be hospitalized for psychiatric emergencies. Some policies will cover this and others exclude it.

Willard B. Frick: Following up Dr. Gromoll's recommendation of a thoughtful analysis of your counseling facilities and services and suggesting that many of us may be making do with stop-gap tactics, I think one of the hopes we had for an outcome of this kind of symposium was that it would stimulate you to think through your counseling needs and start some kind of process for developing a better service.

GROUP B

Psychotherapy with Students

Reported by DAVID PIERCE, *Cornell College*

● *Techniques:*

Our group discussed the possibility of using the relatively new behavior modification techniques. It was recommended that we investigate the use of these techniques, based on learning theory, and there was felt concern and need to stress the point that we evaluate the techniques before we use them, use adequate controls, and follow up and check out the results.

A second matter which was discussed was an extended use of group therapy techniques. In this regard, we found we were all talking about many different things when we said "group therapy." We grouped all these meanings into two broad areas. One might be classified as "restorative," the classical group therapy, where the goal is to restore someone to a functioning level. Another kind of group therapy, and apparently one of growing use, is the "facilitative or sensitivity type training," one in which it is hoped the individual's awareness of others and himself will be enhanced.

A question which follows then is: Is group therapy a treatment of choice in some cases? Frankly, we did not know. Some felt that in some cases it was likely to be a treatment of choice. This deserves investigation—and then we must decide on what basis an individual would be assigned to a group as contrasted with individual treatment.

Nature of the clientele:

In individual instances the members reported that from zero to 35 per cent of your clientele were faculty members. Apparently there is a growing wish for some contact, of some kind, with a psychological service. The question then arises: does the service limit itself to students only?

An additional consideration is that if we see a client for one hour a week, we spend 167 hours of that week outside the therapeutic relationship. There seemed to be a growing wish on the part of the group members to become involved in some way in these other 167 hours. There is a feeling that a psychologist-counselor is now in the position, or wishes to be in the position, of growing out of the psychological isolation, in some place across the campus or down in the basement or wherever you happen to be, and to function as the consultant to the broader community, to the faculty, as well as to the deans and student groups.

There was also a proposal that we consider training programs, of a kind that were discussed in the last period, involving the teaching staff, the resident advisors, chaplains, etc. The possibility of a role conflict, at least as viewed by students, was discussed—when a therapist also functions as a consultant to administration. In this connection it was emphasized that the psychologist-counselor is not a definer of standards and should not place himself in that position.

Funding:

The last point that we discussed has to do with funding, which is totally unrelated to our topic. Some concern was expressed regarding what some people view as a larger sub-population of the total student population which is never reached by psychological services. This condition is present when students are advised by home town physicians to go to this school because they have the kind of service that you need and you can get it faster there, and cheaper there, than we can provide locally. With this in mind our group suggested that off-campus resources, such as foundations or federal funds, be sought in order that these counseling services can be extended. This population, it is felt, is a sub-population of a larger population which includes those destined to be leaders of our country and our communities, and they deserve to be attended to and facilitated to the extent that the community can provide. Another consideration is that the student 2000 miles from his home town cannot be serviced by the agencies, such as county agencies, which could provide services in his home community. We have people from all over the United States and really no money to provide these kinds of services.

COMMENTS AND DISCUSSION

Question: I would like to look into the group insurance for smaller campuses involving off-campus treatment. Dr. Posin, does Brandeis have such a plan?

Dr. Posin: At Brandeis all students have to join our version of Blue Cross or Blue Shield plan which basically pays for hospital service outside our infirmary. This also provides for a certain amount of consultation fee and provides for a certain small amount of payments at a mental hospital which might be necessary for a period of time, or for a series of consultations in an office.

It is my understanding that the way these plans work is that the more people you get into them the better the deal for your money. Taking geography into account, perhaps several small schools could get together and formulate a plan that would cover all of them as one group rather than separately. As I understand it though, you would have to *require* every student to join. This is a bit of a problem, because many are already covered by parents' insurance plans. Premiums for college group plans usually run eleven to twelve dollars a year. In other words, several schools near a mental health center or psychiatrist could think in terms of planning together.

Question: This would suggest the possibility of the associations represented here getting together and working out something—perhaps write to get information on the Brandeis plan, Blue Cross, or national insurance companies.

Willard B. Frick: I would like to pick up the suggestion for use of behavior modification employing learning theory. I personally regard behavior therapy as immoral; however, I would consider this as an excellent program topic for a future meeting. Perhaps an entire day could be planned around different therapeutic techniques with college students. What are the good techniques with students, and what's being done? We could get representatives of this rapidly growing school of thought and practice here as well as representatives of other theories and approaches.

GROUP C

Mental Health Issues on the College Campus

Reported by JOHN LINNELL, *Luther College*

● We went through our possible topics and decided to concentrate on the following four questions:

1. *To what extent are we creating unhealthy pressures through our emphasis on academic excellence?*

In discussing the pressures created by our striving for greater academic excellence, it was pointed out that expectations varied among students. There is the danger of the bright student who comes to college and takes the reading list handed out by the faculty member and feels that he must read every book on the recommended list before Thanksgiving vacation, not being able to deal with the more rational way of choosing among the recommended lists. On the other hand, a study was cited which indicated that students were not really studying all that much, and that most of the pressures came not from the amount of studying that was done, but from the guilt from not studying harder. "Everybody here studies so hard, I don't study hard"—this is the source of the anxiety. However, competition among students, where the emphasis on academic excellence becomes competitive, can make students who don't succeed in the competition feel inadequate. Students need to re-examine their perspectives to identify their myths. At Oberlin when students looked at what actually was done, how their time actually was used, they found that they were not studying all the time. And so the question remains, "When are pressures healthy and under what circumstances are pressures unhealthy?"

2. Do we need to orient parents so they can be more understanding of our educational process?

On this second topic, it was pointed out that the student-parent relationship is often the cause of the emotional problems of our students. The college and the counselor must be very careful not to miscalculate the gap between parents and students and must be very careful not to construct a view of the parent from the conversation with the student. It is important not to limit insight into the parent strictly to the student's perceptions. The counselor must be careful to protect the confidential relationship with students. However, it may be very helpful for the counselor to obtain permission from the student to talk with the parents, letting both parents and students know how the counselor will respond to this discussion with the parents. Various means of communicating with parents were identified: (1) newsletter from the college to the parents, (2) parents weekends on campus, and (3) special orientation meetings for parents (prior to freshmen registration, at registration, and other times throughout the year).

3. What are the characteristics of a healthy climate?

It was generally agreed that there must be an atmosphere of openness among all segments of the academic community; that first attention must be given to the growth of the faculty and administration, for these groups cannot really open up with students if they cannot open up in a meaningful way with themselves; and that initially it is too much really, as a practical matter, to expect faculty to open up with students. You've got to start with just the faculty before you can increase the complexity of the situation by mixing students and faculty and striving to increase openness. At the same time, the recent developments at many colleges have to be encouraged—students need to be involved in a real way in the important decision-making processes of the college. This rather rapid development in higher education is very, very good. Then there was considerable discussion about the possibility of our conceding that maybe we can learn something from business and adopt the program of sensitivity training which has worked in business and industry. Not the notion of taking your whole faculty and having a man in for one day and thinking you're going to make any impact on the campus community, but starting with the president and the people the president has to work with. A solid two-week program working with some of these skilled people could have the potential for significantly altering the campus community for the better.

4. *Where do students seek help?*

It was pointed out that students can be effective listeners, and it is desirable for us to recognize this and at the same time assist students to recognize their own limits so they don't get scared off and try to handle something they can't handle. We need to recognize that being sympathetic, being a "brother" to the student, can be helpful and it's not necessary for us to say, "Gee, you better go talk to someone else about this." We were fortunate enough to have Dr. Jourard in our group and he pointed out that at the University of Florida Health Service they have learned from experience that many students are good listeners, have good common sense, they work well with other students—and they actually refer students to students. With a student having a given kind of a problem they might suggest, "Why don't you go talk to John Jones over in the dormitory—you might find this would be useful." They have found that this is a helpful way of using students, i.e., to counsel other students. We were concerned with possible ways or mechanics for creating a helping atmosphere in the total college. A suggestion arose, again from the University of Florida, one of those wild suggestions that we'd like to try sometime just to see what would happen. This is that perhaps we could work out a way in which students would be asked to identify things they were good at, things in which they would be willing to help other students. Thus they might help other students invited to a dance but who don't know how to dance, or who need to learn how to handle a particular problem in chemistry, or how to arrange things for a certain program. Maybe we could structure some way of finding students who are willing to help students at specific things and put them in contact with each other. And again we need to continually look for ways in which faculty can be with students in any informal and open way. All of us are familiar enough with the genuine and valuable contacts between students and faculty to try to find some way of encouraging this without killing it with formalized structure.

COMMENTS AND DISCUSSION

Joseph C. Heston: On the lobby table you will find copies of the report (BIRC Research Report #87) on how our students at Albion rate their faculty counselors. This report covers some of the things you have been talking about, e.g. what kinds of problems they will take to their faculty counselors, what kind of problems they will take to students, and how they rate the effectiveness of these sources of help.

Willard B. Frick: Two groups have covered the topic of confidentiality. I would just like to say that one of our keynote speakers, Dr. Patterson, has done some of the best writing on this issue of any person that I've read. I would recommend his books for his statements and discussion of the issue of confidentiality; they are quite good. Group C emphasized that in order to achieve a more viable and healthy climate on the campus there needs to be more openness among administrators, faculty, and students. They also brought in the topic of T-groups. There is an interest among some faculty groups on our campus to become involved for, say, an extended weekend in a "sensitivity" or "basic encounter" group. We hope to work something out for this group of faculty during this school year. I think it offers a tremendous possibility, if used right and with proper leadership, for creating such openness.

GROUP D

Prevention: Techniques and Programs

Reported by WILLIAM CRAFTS, *Monmouth College*

● It seems that much of our work overlapped that of Group C and what they discussed. But we have our share of platitudes and admonitions to voice as well. In our discussion of prevention we agreed that the environment was all-important, more important than the sum total of individual programs and efforts to aid in the preventive task. We saw the environment as a growing, changing, dynamic thing in which people learn and develop. In many ways we were saying to one another that we had to encourage fresh air blowing through the institution now and then and to prevent what John Gardner has referred to as "institutional dry rot."

During the first session we looked at our task as a two-sided one: first we talked about promotion of certain conditions and results, and then we went on to prevention of certain results or conditions. And I might just list these briefly for you:

A. *Promotion of desirable conditions, results, or outcomes within the environment.*

   1. Academic potential on the part of individual students.
   2. Personal development, development of personal powers, abilities, talents.
   3. Certain "liberating" results, such as the development of flexibility or creativity on the part of individuals.
   4. The ability to cope with stress, the ability of individuals to live with stress.
   5. Providing of varied adult role models, on the part of faculty

and administration, to aid students in the natural process of exploration and development.

6. The opportunity for varied small group memberships, to encourage students to affiliate with others in a small group arrangement for individual benefit.

7. Flexible curricular arrangements, as a desirable outcome or condition in our institutions. For example, independent study, off-campus study, and the like. We find this to be a highly desirable thing to promote.

8. Institutional concern in our relationships, or a dialogic function which we should promote. This means open discussion, a free flourishing type of discussion with students about their true concerns at every level. This means, of course, an institutional flexibility on our part, a willingness to examine ourselves, or to get into any kind of issue, no matter where it may lead us.

9. The promotion of an ability to live within structures, with controls, imposed from without and from within.

B. *Conditions and results to be prevented.*

1. Undue and unnecessary stress.
2. Unrealistic expectations of students, brought with them when they come, and retained.
3. Being overwhelmed by the academic system, its demands, and being frustrated by such, without relief.
4. Instances of outright pathology or maladjustment.

C. *Specific instances of prevention in action.*

Many of these have to do with the actual engagement of all of us in an institutional community with one another on timely and important issues, full engagement without holding back, as has been emphasized so well throughout this symposium.

1. Students having membership on faculty committees of all types to study salient campus issues.
2. Efforts to spark action within the campus community, again a matter of faculty and students working openly together, to infuse light into stagnant structures or committees.
3. Setting up ad hoc faculty-student committees to attack timely

issues as they arise, or perhaps before they develop to a dangerous point.

4. The continual face-to-face confrontation between students, faculty, and administration for a productive kind of interaction and communication. We feel this kind of confrontation should develop at all levels.

5. Retreats, as helpful and as preventive: retreats for the entire community, if that is possible, or for certain segments of the academic community for some meaningful dialogue.

6. Mental health lectures on the lively topics that concern students, speaking to their interest at the time that the interest must be explored.

7. The role of campus media. Here we felt that there must be some provision for segments of the campus to speak out on issues, to explore one another's thinking.

8. Use of reports, e.g. on low scholarship, from faculty members to the dean's office and on to residence hall counselors so that residence hall staff could meet in individual groups with students who were having academic problems.

9. Orientation and training sessions for staff and residence hall counselors.

10. Individual consultations, staff members or resident counselors, to meet with college psychiatrist or college health service in order to discuss a person's problem.

11. Student-student contacts, the possibilities of such things as "big sister" and "big brother" programs.

12. Summer registration and counseling, as another way of providing a more adequate expectation of college for entering students.

13. Student-initiated discussions with faculty and staff, perhaps about academic or curriculum matters that have flared into the open.

D. *Fundamental institution needs:*

1. Continual and realistic assessment of behavior and conditions existing within the academic community.

2. Full, open communications at all levels, from one individual to another, from individual to group, etc.

3. Opportunity for genuine engagement in the life of the college community, as opposed to a stilted or limited kind of involvement,

of all persons based on respect for one another and a desire to understand one another better.

4. Strive for increased sensitivity to student needs.

In brief, we should say to our students (and mean it): "We're very glad you're here, and we want to do our best to help you to achieve and develop within the academic community through a vital kind of engagement that we can have here."

COMMENTS AND DISCUSSION

No comments or discussion following Group D.

GROUP E

"New Morality" on the Campus

Reported by ALICE LOW, *Grinnell College*

● First let me review some comments made yesterday by Dr. Rutledge in our group after his main talk. According to him, the basic problems of young people have really not changed over the last twenty years; at least this is what he has seen in pre-marital counseling. There is still a great taboo against tenderness. Sex taken out of context of human relationships is still extremely damaging. Young people talk a great deal about sex, but they are still seeking, in many honest ways, basic understandings of human relationships. And, of course, this then becomes a challenge to us in what we are doing specifically on our own campuses in helping to meet that need. Dr. Rutledge discussed in some detail the great need for in-service training, for very close communication among staff and among faculty. He was talking about their attempts, at Merrill-Palmer, to have interdisciplinary training of staff members as well as to have the staff members with their own particular skill in one theory. Only an infinitesimal amount of pre-marital counseling is actually being done in the country today. On college campuses we find that most of this is being done incidentally, and not in a planned program. The present professional psychiatric training actually seems to discourage the working of a psychiatrist with two people, such as one would have with the marriage relationship. Therefore, he has difficulty making referrals of patients to other people who would be competent in dealing with them in either pre-marital or marital relationships. The best investment in the health of our children really is to treat their parents. He feels that every campus with 800 students needs at least one trained full-time counselor or psychotherapist, and probably then for every additional 300 students there should be either a part-time or full-time staff member, depending on the situation. The question is now being raised on liberal arts campuses as to how we can provide better training and information for our students in relationship to pre-marital counseling. The suggestion was made that in addition to the professional people who are being made available on campuses, it is also possible that much of the pertinent material could be incorporated in any developmental course in psychology.

This morning we tried to develop our own committee report. Rather than primarily discuss sexual morality, we confined our remarks to broad social issues.

Group E feels we should really be addressing ourselves to these pertinent questions:

1. There should be a more extensive application of psychodynamics to the basic social issues.

2. Problems among underprivileged or minority groups have many similarities, educationally and sociologically. This certainly has implications for our future programs. For instance, Dr. Rutledge explained that they were finding many similar characteristics among the disadvantaged Negroes of Detroit and Chicago areas and the disadvantaged whites in the same areas and also in the Appalachians. Some of this will certainly be applicable to future programs.

3. Social issues on our own campuses:

a) Discrimination in membership in sororities and fraternities has not appreciably changed on many college campuses, and what are we specifically doing about it? The important thing is, if you have sororities and fraternities, is progress being made in the kind of discrimination that has previously taken place, or is it only a "token" kind of acknowledgment?

b) A new minority group power syndrome is becoming much more apparent on college campuses. What are the implications of this movement and how are we prepared to work with it? In other words, we are seeing now the organization of minority groups, particularly Negroes, in what is becoming a small (and in some cases a rather large) power structure. There seems to be an expressed need and desire on the part of the minority group to band together for whatever purposes, rather than an inclination to join with other kinds of organized groups or work with existing structures.

c) What special attention, if any, is being given to disadvantaged groups? What kind of an evaluation do we have of our programs? Are we fully recognizing the depth of major cultural differences, or do we make many invalid assumptions about the kinds of things we are doing with these people? For instance, on some campuses lists were made available to faculty members of students that were actually considered as "high risks" on the campus. Other campuses were simply not making any special issues of this at all; but tutorial programs and financial assistance were available if the need were expressed. Certainly there are many ways of approaching this. But the question is raised, "What are you doing and what are you seeing in the way that you are doing it?"

d) Drugs: Recognition was made of the number of colleges who have taken the positive steps of official drug statements and are working with an educational program. Questions were raised in regard to this issue:

(1) What do we project for the next few years?

(2) How are we working, if at all, with civil authorities?

(3) How well informed are our students? What are we doing to make them better informed?

(4) Have we defined clearly the role of the institution during these particular years of experimentation? In other words, do the students really know where the college stands as an institution in relation to drug usage? Do the students know where they can go to get assistance?

e) Has your institution made it clear to all members of its community the expectation for students in their social lives and in the area of human relationships? Are these expectations clear to the institution and/or the students? This position could be established in many different ways, but it should be through the co-operative effort of students, faculty, and administration.

We are all in similar situations of re-evaluating whatever our structure is, and hopefully we will be re-evaluating it every year. The question is: How great is the involvement of the constituents of your community and how constructively can they be involved?

COMMENT

Perhaps the high risk students should not be called the "High Risk Students," but rather the "Big Betters," because they are the ones who are gambling, not we! I suggest, if we say anything to the faculty at all, that we say, "These are the kids on this campus that are betting the most, with the worst odds, so it isn't *we* who are risking, but *they* [the students] who are risking." I think it might change attitudes!

APPENDIX

Participants in the Symposium

EDITORS AND SYMPOSIUM DIRECTORS

JOSEPH C. HESTON, Ph.D., Director of Bureau of Institutional Research and Counseling and Professor of Psychology, Albion College, Albion, Michigan. Dr. Heston received his Ph.D. in Clinical Psychology at the Ohio State University in 1941. He is a Fellow of the American Psychological Association and a Diplomate in Counseling Psychology of the American Board of Examiners in Professional Psychology (1948). Dr. Heston has been a psychology professor and counseling director at DePauw University and Fresno State College before coming to Albion College in 1955. He served as Chairman of the Department of Psychology at Albion College before organizing the Bureau of Institutional Research and Counseling in 1963. Dr. Heston has been visiting professor on the staff of N.D.E.A. Guidance and Counseling Institutes at Ohio University (1960-63). In 1965 he was Fulbright Senior Lecturer in counseling psychology at Australian National University, Canberra, Australia. He is the author of some twenty journal articles and the *Heston Personal Adjustment Inventory* (Harcourt, Brace and World, 1949), *How to Take a Test* (Science Research Associates, 1952), and *Learning About Tests* (Science Research Associates, 1955).

WILLARD B. FRICK, M.A., College Counselor, Bureau of Institutional Research and Counseling, and Assistant Professor of Psychology, Albion College, Albion, Michigan. Professor Frick earned his M.A. in Psychology at George Peabody College (1952) and is completing his Ph.D. in Educational Psychology at the University of Michigan. He did an internship in counseling and psychotherapy at Merrill-Palmer Institute (1959-60). Mr. Frick was a visiting professor in the N.D.E.A. Counseling and Guidance Institutes at Western Michigan University (1962-63). He has served as a psychology professor at Simpson College, Bridgewater College, and Arkansas State College before coming to Albion in 1963. Mr. Frick has been a school psychologist and research assistant. In 1955-56 he was a Fulbright Exchange Teacher, North Riding College, Scarborough, England. In addition to numerous journal articles, he is co-author (with Frank Womer) of *Personalizing Test Use: A Counselor's Casebook*, Ann Arbor: University of Michigan, 1965. Mr. Frick is also editor of *Explorations in Healthy Personality* (currently in press, Pitman Publishing Company).

AUTHORS OF MAJOR ADDRESSES

EDWARD S. BORDIN, Ph.D., Professor of Psychology and Chief of the Counseling Division, Bureau of Psychological Services, University of Michigan. Dr. Bordin obtained the doctorate from Ohio State University in 1942. Prior to joining the University of Michigan faculty in 1948, he was involved in research and counseling at Ohio State University and was Assistant Professor of Psychology at the University of Minnesota. From 1946-48 Dr. Bordin served as Director of the Student Counseling Center at State College of Washington. Dr. Bordin's book publication is *Psychological Counseling*, Appleton-Century-Crofts, 1955. His extensive bibliography includes work in counseling and psychotherapy, personality development, and development of vocational interests. Dr. Bordin's range of contributions to the field of counseling includes service on important committees of the American Psychological Association, including Chairman of the Education and Training Board. In 1964 he was elected Chairman of the Board of Professional Affairs. Dr. Bordin also served for several years as editor of the *Journal of Consulting Psychology*. The second edition of his book, *Psychological Counseling*, will be published in 1968.

SIDNEY M. JOURARD, Ph.D., Professor of Psychology, University of Florida, Gainesville, Florida. Canadian by birth, Dr. Jourard received his Doctorate in Psychology from the University of Buffalo, Buffalo, New York, in 1953. He has held professorships at the University of Buffalo, Emory University, and the University of Alabama Medical College. He has held his present position at the University of Florida since 1958. During most of his career he has been active in the private practice of psychotherapy. Dr. Jourard's publications include four books: *Personal Adjustment: An Approach Through the Study of Healthy Personality*, Macmillan, 1958, second edition, 1963; *The Transparent Self*, Van Nostrand, 1964; and *Reconciliation: A Theory of Psychological Growth*, Van Nostrand, 1967 (editor of the posthumous book of F. J. Shaw); and *Disclosing Man to Himself*, Van Nostrand, 1968. Dr. Jourard has also published in a variety of professional journals including: *Journal of Consulting Psychology, Journal of Humanistic Psychology, Journal of Existential Psychiatry*, and *Review of Existential Psychology and Psychiatry*. Much of Dr. Jourard's writing and research in recent years has been devoted to the development of the concept of self-disclosure and its relationship to positive mental health or healthy personality. Dr. Jourard is a Past President of the

American Association for Humanistic Psychology and he serves on the Board of Editors for the *Journal of Humanistic Psychology*.

LESTER A. KIRKENDALL, Ph.D., Professor of Family Life at Oregon State University, Corvallis, Oregon. Dr. Kirkendall's doctorate was completed at Columbia University. He has taught at the Teachers College of Connecticut, the University of Oklahoma, served in the United States Office of Education, and is a Past Director of the Association for Family Living in Chicago. He was a recent Visiting Professor at the University of Kansas Medical Center where he worked with student doctors and nurses in the areas of sex education and family life. Dr. Kirkendall has lectured and published widely. He has written numerous chapters in books, articles for a wide variety of journals, and is the author of eight books including *Pre-Marital Intercourse and Interpersonal Relationships*, Julian Press, 1961. Much of Dr. Kirkendall's current writing and lecturing is devoted to his interest in interpersonal relationships as a framework for value judgments and decision making in human relations situations. Dr. Kirkendall is also in frequent counseling contact with young people caught up in the moral and ethical dilemmas of our age.

C. H. PATTERSON, Ph.D., Professor of Educational Psychology, and Chairman, Division of Counseling and Guidance, University of Illinois, Urbana, Illinois. Dr. Patterson received his Ph.D. degree in Educational Psychology in 1955 from the University of Minnesota. During his distinguished career he has taught at Antioch College and held a variety of positions at the University of Minnesota. He was a Clinical Psychologist with the United States Army, and following World War II he served for several years as Counseling Psychologist for the Veterans Administration. Dr. Patterson is a prolific and versatile writer, having published over one hundred articles and numerous book reviews since 1941. He is also the author of twelve books including his most recent publications: *Theories of Counseling and Psychotherapy*, Harper & Row, 1966; and *The Counselor in the School: Selected Readings*, McGraw-Hill, 1967. In his professional work at the University of Illinois, Dr. Patterson is widely known for his work in counselor training.

AUTHORS OF PANEL PRESENTATIONS

MILTON CUDNEY, Ph.D., Associate Professor of Education and Staff Member of the Counseling Center, Western Michigan University, Kalamazoo, Michigan.

ALBERT DAVISON, M.A., Director of Student Employment, Placement, and Institutional Research, Denison University, Granville, Ohio.

WESTON MORRILL, Ph.D., Assistant Professor of Education and Associate Director, University Counseling Center, Colorado State University, Fort Collins, Colorado.

HERBERT POSIN, M.D., Director, Mental Health Services, Brandeis University, Waltham, Massachusetts. Associate Clinical Professor of Psychiatry, Boston University School of Medicine.

LAWRENCE RIGGS, Ed.D., Dean of Students, and Professor of Psychology, The College of Wooster, Wooster, Ohio. Well known for work in alcohol education.

WILLIAM R. ROGERS, Ph.D., Associate Professor of Psychology and Religion and Associate Dean of the College, Earlham College, Richmond, Indiana. Post-doctoral study at the Tavistock Clinic and Institute of Human Relations, London, England.

AARON L. RUTLEDGE, Th.D., Director of the Psychotherapy Program at the Merrill-Palmer Institute, Detroit, Michigan. Author of a recent text, *Pre-Marital Counseling*, Schenkman, 1966.

JOHN THOMPSON, Ph.D., Associate Professor and Clinical Psychologist in Oberlin College Psychological Services, Oberlin, Ohio. Dr. Thompson is a Diplomate of the American Board of Examiners in Professional Psychology.

FRANK B. WOMER, Ph.D., Professor of Education and Consultant in Testing and Guidance, Bureau of School Services, The University of Michigan. Author of over two dozen important articles and bulletins on educational testing and measurement. Co-author of *Personalizing Test Use: A Counselor's Casebook* (with Willard B. Frick), Ann Arbor: The University of Michigan, 1965.

OTHER PARTICIPANTS

GREAT LAKES COLLEGES ASSOCIATION

Albion College
Charles Leeds, Dean of Students
Carolyn Jones, Dean of Women
Louis W. Norris, President

Antioch College
Phil McQueen, Director of Counseling
Walter W. Sikes, Dean of Students

Denison University
Donald Tritt, Director of Psychological Clinic

DePauw University
    William McK. Wright, Dean of Students
    Richard Kelly, Director of the Bureau of Testing and Research
    Miss Nell Barnhart, Associate Dean of Students

Earlham College
    Wallace Mealiea, Director of Student Counseling

Hope College
    Robert S. Brown, Director of Counseling Center

Kalamazoo College
    J. Douglas Hickerson, Assistant Dean of Men

Kenyon College
    Rowland H. Shepard, College Counselor
    Thomas J. Edwards, Dean of Students

Oberlin College
    George H. Langeler, Dean of Students
    Mrs. Anita Reichard, Dean of Women

Ohio Wesleyan University
    Margaret Forsythe, Dean of Women
    Ronald S. Stead, Dean of Men

Wabash College
    W. H. Davis, M.D., Psychiatric Counselor
    John Lawrie, Psychology Department

The College of Wooster
    Mrs. Carolyn Dix, Dean of Women
    Ralph Young, Dean of Men

Associated Colleges of the Midwest

Beloit College
    William Dreffin, College Counselor
    John P. Gwin, Dean of Students

Carleton College
    William Kirtner, College Counselor and Associate Professor of Psychology
    Daniel K. Van Eyck, Dean of Students

Coe College
    Unable to send a representative.

PARTICIPANTS

Cornell College
    David Pierce, College Counselor
Grinnell College
    Mrs. Alice Low, Dean of Women
    Dennis Haas, College Chaplain

Knox College
    Gary S. Isaacson, College Counselor
    Ivan C. Harlan, Dean of Students

Lawrence University
    Francis L. Broderick, Dean of Lawrence and Downer Colleges
    Curtis W. Tarr, President

Monmouth College
    William Crafts, Dean of Students
    Paul McClanahan, College Chaplain

Ripon College
    David Harris, Dean of Men and Associate Professor of Psychology
    Jean Van Hergel, Dean of Women
    Robert Wilson, Assistant Academic Dean

St. Olaf College
    Henry M. Helgen, Jr., Dean of Students
    Theodore Hilpert, College Counselor

CENTRAL STATES COLLEGE ASSOCIATION

Alma College
    Thomas Plough, Dean of Student Affairs
    John Kimball, Vice President for Administrative Services

Augustana College
    James C. Ribbeck, Dean of Men
    Francis C. Gamelin, Vice President for Academic Affairs and Dean of the College
    Miss Betsey Brodahl, Dean of Women

Carroll College
    C. W. Cook, Dean of Men
    Jane Swan, Dean of Women

Gustavus Adolphus College
    William Lydecker, Director of Counseling
    Robert C. Butler, Dean of Student Affairs

Illinois Wesleyan University
    Miss Anne H. Meierhofer, Dean of Students
    Jerry Jensen, Dean of Men

Luther College
    C. G. Kloster, Vice President for Student Affairs
    John Linnell, Vice President for Academic Affairs and Dean
    E. O. Naeseth, Dean of Students

MacMurray College
    Phoebe E. Wilkins, Counseling Coordinator
    James Stefl, Dean of Men
    Miss Martha Robbins, Dean of Women

Manchester College
    Russell V. Bollinger, Dean of Students
    A. Blair Helman, President

Millikin University
    Henry Gromoll, Consulting Psychologist
    Byron L. Kerns, Dean of Students
    Paul L. McKay, President

Mundelein College
    Mrs. Sylvia Warshaw, Director of Counseling Services
    Sister Irene M. Meyer, Chairman, Department of Psychology
    Sister Mary A. Cramer, Dean of Students

St. John's College
    Rev. Finian McDonald, Assistant Director of Counseling
    Rev. Anthony Hellenberg, Assistant Chaplain

Simpson College
    Walter B. Wiser, Dean of Students